COPYWRITING

The ultimate guide to learning how to write copy that sells, communicate with impact, write persuasive advertising, generate quick cash and take your business on the next level

CONTENTS

Introduction

INTRODUCTION

A freelance copywriter is any individual who produces substance or content on interest. The 'freelance' indicates that they work as a free operator, for the most part doing unmistakably limited copywriting tasks or commissions on an impromptu premise and for a scope of customers. 'Copywriter' is an approximately characterized term, since copywriting often incorporates a range of errands that might be significantly more unequivocally characterized in different businesses, (for example, distributing): composing, changing, organizing, arranging, altering, duplicate altering, editing and contact with a scope of different experts, for example, visual fashioners and web designers.

When they work with organizations, copywriters offer help to the showcasing capacity by composing promoting materials, for example, handouts, ads, and websites. Ordinarily, the freelance copywriter will manage the advertising administrator or showcasing director, although in a little firm the MD or CEO may approach the freelance copywriter direct.

Freelance copywriters additionally work with offices, where they bolster the creative work of the office by adding a copywriting capacity to their administration portfolio. While many organizations offer composition administrations, they may utilize a freelance to do the actual work - either because they do not have the limit with regards to copywriting in-house or because they need the aptitudes of a specific copywriter.

Freelance copywriters additionally work with different sorts of the customer - open division associations, philanthropies, scholastics - any individual who needs something composed may be keen on the administrations of a copywriter.

Many freelance copywriters list their administrations in conventional directories, much the same as some other business. In any case, for by far most, the critical method for connecting up with new customers is through the web. Most copywriters currently have their web presences, often enhanced for web crawlers with the goal that they can draw in web clients who enter terms, for example, 'copywriter' or 'freelance copywriter.' To lessen rivalry, they may likewise look to rank for phrases, for example, 'copywriter Norwich' or 'copywriter London.' To develop the profile of their webpage, copywriters may look for inclusion in web-based copywriting directories, for example, these precedents at Yahoo and FreeIndex.

When contact has been made, the freelance copywriter meets with the customer to figure out what sort of copywriting is required. This implies thinking about such significant angles as reason, manner of speaking, target format, and (in particular) the circumstance of the per-user and the reaction that the copywriter is planning to inspire from them. Great copywriters will cautiously assemble this information before starting their copywriting.

Before starting work, the freelance copywriter will try to concur a cost with their customer. Most copywriters charge continuously, although some may consent to charge regularly, or (for certain kinds of commission) by the word or thousand words. Charging by the word conveys the hazard that many revisions will be required to get the duplicate right, leaving the copywriter undercharging. In any case, for certain errands, (for example, the production of a lot of web crawler well-disposed duplicate), the per-word premise might be fitting.

A practical gauge of time prerequisites is fundamental, and the customer needs to acknowledge how much work can go into a freelance copywriting commission. For instance, the making of a three-word trademark may include a few days of liaising with company executives, auditing contenders' substance, conceptualizing, and assessment.

Many copywriters work without a full, legitimately restricting contract set up. While not perfect, there are many reasons why they may do this. Above all else is the longing to satisfy the customer by continuing ahead with the original composition as opposed to getting tied up an arrangement. Regardless, an email from the customer to the freelance copywriter with explicit authorization to continue is generally sufficient reason for the copywriter to start work.

Chapter one

The universal hidden structure behind all persuasive copy

The headline is one of the two most critical leverage points in any direct mail advertisement or promotion. (The other is the offer.) A solid headline can have a considerable effect in affecting your prospect to keep perusing. Thus, it's critical to have a reliable, compelling headline.

This part arrangement covers seven critical tips for composing great, enticing headlines that maneuver your peruser into your body duplicate. Utilize these tips as a guide for making a headline... what's more, as a test to decide the quality it.

Headline Tip #1: Flag Your Target Audience

I make a distinction between your objective market and your intended interest group. Your accurate market speaks to the total number of potential prospects for your product or administration. It is characterized by specific common attributes with your current purchasers.

Your intended interest group, then again, is the subset of that gathering who are well on the way to purchase from you. This speaks to your "destitute group," and is the objective you're going for. For instance, when you pitch a product to help individuals quit smoking, your objective market might be smokers who need to stop... your intended interest group will doubtlessly be smokers who so urgently need to finish they are eager to attempt your answer, even though nothing else has worked for them. There's an unpretentious however vital distinction here that can have a significant effect on your outcomes.

You can hail your gathering of people either unequivocally or verifiable. For instance, if you were to cheer your group of onlookers unequivocally, you may turn out and state, "Consideration: Smokers Who Desperately Want To Quit..."

On the other hand, you can be somewhat more "smooth" by indeed hailing your crowd this way: "Acquainting A Scientifically-Proven Method With Help Smokers Quit Cold-Turkey WITHOUT The Intense Cravings. Ensured To Get You Over The 'Mound' Or Your Money Back."

When hailing your gathering of people, it's critical to have a comprehension of their identity, what most impacts them, and what issues they're anxious about.

The ideal approach to discover is to chat with your purchasers face to face. You are meeting them to find out what they were experiencing when they purchased your product. You'll be shocked at what you reveal! I ensure what you realize will help make your headline, yet the majority of your duplicate significantly more potent and concentrated on your intended interest group.

Headline Tip #2: Be Unique

One sign of a powerless headline is anybody selling a similar arrangement could utilize it. Assume the weight loss market, for instance. "Get more fit Now" is not an exceptionally great headline because there is nothing one of a kind about it. Anybody selling any weight-loss product could utilize it.

Then again, the accompanying headline is substantially more powerful...

"Step by step instructions to Melt Your Fat Away And Keep It Off For Good Using This Little-Known Detox Secret The Diet Industry Doesn't Want You To Know About..."

Copywriting Tips - Persuasive Copywriting - Is There Any Other Kind?

If you're duplicate isn't enticing, can it indeed be called copywriting or is its content? The general purpose of copywriting is to compose deals copy that outcomes in more transformations.

Influence is the capacity to move somebody to a strategy, and that is actually what copywriting ought to do, isn't that so? Persuasive copywriting is in this way a repetitive expression for copywriting is enticing ordinarily, or it's no longer copywriting.

From the title to the third PS at the base of your business page, your whole spotlight with every word on the page is to influence the peruser to go in the ideal direction - more often than not a deal. To do this, what you truly need to concentrate on is the peruser.

When your duplicate is about what they need and need, you will evoke genuine emotion in the peruser that will make them ask to purchase from you.

The extremely skilled marketing specialist does all that while never coming appropriate out and saying, "Hello, you, you have to purchase this." Instead, he will begin by recounting a tale about himself or another person that features the pessimistic feelings related to whatever the product will settle.

This draws in the per-user and gets them to harp a bit on the painful aspects of whatever the issue is. At the point when you complete the story with how marvel it felt when the product tackled the problem, the per-user needs to feel the equivalent.

The best influence is the point at which we induce ourselves, and that is the thing that a decent publicist can do. He will utilize words to inspire an enthusiastic reaction and the creative energy of the peruser. When he does that, the peruser will offer himself.

Copywriting Tips - 5 Qualities of a Good Brochure

Indeed, even with a sophisticated nonstop web presence, e-bulletins, web journals, and other online gadgets, brochures (and brochure publicists) keep on assuming an essential job in marketing. There are lastingness and transportability to a printed copy brochure; and brochures will, in general, be perused and alluded to at an alternate pace to web content, which implies that sophisticated messages and contentions can be grown quickly. What's more, when an elegantly composed and perfectly structured brochure drops through a letter-box, it has an effect that no website can ever accomplish. Anyway, with regards to copywriting tips, what are the five critical copywriting characteristics of a decent brochure?

- Each brochure should be objective-driven
- A decent pamphlet recounts to a story.
- Connecting with brochures offset influence with data
- Brochure duplicate must work in an organization with structure.
- It's essential to get the brochure's manner of speaking right.
- Brochure copywriting should dependably be objective-driven

From Gloucester, the UK to Gloucester, Massachusetts, marketing spending plans are valuable, and each penny must work successfully for brands. Likewise, with any marketing activity, brochure copywriting ought to dependably be driven by a clear goal. What do you need your brochure to accomplish and for whom? It's necessary, and it's essential to the achievement of your marketing security.

A brochure should recount an applicable story.

A brochure should recount a story as the publicist takes the peruser on a sturdy, enlightening, and significant voyage from the intro page to the last suggestion to take action. That story will be created by your brochure destinations and the key messages that you concur with your publicist.

Talented brochure journalists balance influence and data

Great brochure marketing specialists dependably accentuate benefits. Data alone, whether product features or administration offers, is good for nothing except if customers can comprehend what it implies for them. This typically boils down to setting aside cash, sparing time and fabricating or ensuring notorieties. Deliberately created enticing contentions, allied to irresistible customer benefits, lie at the core of fruitful brochure substance composing. For a brochure or some other marketing producing, concentrating on customer benefits consistently emerges as one of the top copywriting tips.

In a decent brochure, duplicate works in organization with brochure plan.

Leave brochure structure to novices and the outcome is typically over-burden pages, poor arranging and not well thought about cooperation between duplicate, pictures, and design. An image might merit a thousand words, at the end of the day, it's words that convince. Copywriting and posters should work in an organization, with each having space to inhale amid a lot of blank areas. The best brochure copywriting is structured related to the brochure's visual computerization; gifted brochure authors get this.

It's essential to get the brochure's manner of speaking right.

While a similar essential message can be conveyed from numerous points of view, the decision of conveyance can have an enormous effect on how your business is seen. Manner of speaking will be driven by your image and the messages and qualities that you wish to impart to your intended interest groups. From the unpretentious pitch to a punchy 'in your face' approach; from energetically captivating to moderate and definitive, manner of speaking is the manner in which your business talks: cautious thought of the selection of words, the utilization (or shirking) of explicit expressions; their conveyance and even their design on the brochure page are exceedingly significant. A decent brochure publicist will comprehend your image and help you use the manner of speaking to depict your business in the way that you need.

Goals, narrating, parity, structure, and manner of speaking. Joining these brochure copywriting characteristics effectively is a specific aptitude. Do you or your group genuinely have that ability? Also, do you have sufficient energy to do your own copywriting? With such a significant amount in question, including right correspondence of your indispensable business message, a standout amongst the essential copywriting tips could be to contract an accomplished brochure marketing specialist.

10 Website Copywriting Tips

Powerful search motor enhanced (SEO) Website copywriting can tremendously affect your deals and showcasing. Here are 10 Website copywriting tips to make a progressively successful Website and drastically improve how you work together on the web:

1. Keyword research: This is stage one of Website copywriting. There are numerous excellent free and paid administrations online that you can use to recognize what terms your intended interest group is searching to discover your rivals on the web. Directed keyword research in addition to crucial SEO Website copywriting equivalents preferred search rankings over your opposition on Google and other search engines.

2. Feature: The feature is number two on my rundown. However, it's central for SEO Website copywriting. You completely should incorporate your keyword in the function. When you don't, it resembles setting up an "Available to be purchased" sign without expressing what's available to be purchased. For example, if you had a 2008 Black Honda Accord available to be bought your sign yet said, "Vehicle available to be purchased," what amount would you say you are not conveying?

3. Keyword placement: notwithstanding the feature, your essential keyword ought to show up in the first or two sentences, be sprinkled all through the copy however much as could reasonably be expected without diverting from your message, and be incorporated towards the finish of the page.

4. Landing page copy: This is the place we see probably the most issues with Website copywriting. You've without a doubt seen locales with two sentences on the landing page, just as destinations with a large number of words on the landing page. The two systems are fruitless. Too little copy doesn't take into account keywords to be utilized and doesn't induce a guest to make a move. A lot of text can weaken essential keywords, and typically drills a guest into clicking far from the webpage rapidly a one-two punch when you consider your Website copywriting objective was to draw in the potential client to your website with essential keywords and after that constrain him/her to make some move.

5. Convincing copy: "For what reason am I here, and for what reason do I give it a second thought?" People are occupied. Regardless of how incredible your site looks (put every one of the fancy odds and ends on it if you like) if the copy isn't drawing in they will in all respects rapidly proceed onward to a contender's site. It's that basic.

6. Slugs: This is a regularly disregarded part of Website copywriting. The search engines focus on shots since they get out significant things, so incorporate a keyword or two in your projectiles too. Shots separate lumps of copy and make data simpler to process. Since many Web clients are skimmers, they may peruse the balls in any case, so ensure you incorporate critical advantages of your items and administrations.

7. Client-centered copy: "How might this benefit me?" Visitors to your Website couldn't care less about you. It's the harsh truth. They care about your answers to their issues. Your Website copywriting needs to mirror this reality. How does your item/administration advantage them? Do they set aside cash? Time? Get a special item? Individual administration? Give them the advantages before the highlights in your Website copywriting, and they'll be bound to make a move.

8. Subheads: Are your keywords in your subheads? The search engines recognize keywords in subheads to be increasingly significant and, similar to projectiles, convincing subheads to help separate the copy.

9. Solid suggestion to take action: Your copywriting isn't finished without a convincing invitation to take action. Regardless of whether it's approaching the guest to get in touch with you for more data or to buy an item on your site, the suggestion to take action needs to explicitly state what you need them to do in a manner that helps them to remember the advantages of your items/administrations.

10. Metadata: After you've finished your Website copywriting, make sure to give your Web programmer/designer with the meta title, meta depiction, and keywords to incorporate into the code for the search engines.

There's as yet one inquiry you have to pose to yourself: What do I need my Website to achieve? Make sense of that, and you'll know your Website copywriting procedure.

Convincing and Professional Power Copywriting Tips for the Web and SEO

Inspirational Triggers that Make People Buy

Inside this section on business copywriting systems, we will see how to structure your copywriting when functioning for a customer. There has been a lot of copywriting done during that time, and it isn't essential to reevaluate the wheel each time you need to compose duplicate. We will explicitly be engaged upon the sales letter since this could have the best effect for you, particularly if you choose to do SEO copywriting.

One specific school of thought addresses making your site one large online sales letter. Proceeding in this line of reasoning, this could display an extraordinary open door for you. You could compose for both disconnected organizations just as for online business utilizing the configuration of a sales letter.

Inside a sales letter, three main segments will have any effect on whether your item will sell.

The first segment is the feature.

When you don't catch your prospects' eye immediately, you will have squandered your time in building up the remainder of the duplicate.

The second part of a sales letter is the offer.

This part is significant as you should be express with the idea to give the prospect what the person in question presently needs. It must be something that will allure the opportunity to make a move upon the culmination of perusing the letter.

The last part of a sales letter is the postscript.

This is the second most perused segment of a sales letter after the feature. When you are composing this, this is the additional motivator that you will utilize inspire your prospects to exploit the offer that you displayed immediately. When you are centering after composition a sales letter, you should make every specific stride of the sales letter altogether. You don't plunk down and composes a sales letter totally through but instead, make it stride by step. This involves writing the feature pursued by writing the offer and after that pursued by arranging the postscript.

Following these copywriting methodology will guarantee that you will have set yourself up for extraordinary achievement.

When you don't have a lot of understanding inside copywriting, make a point to pursue the instances of copywriting systems set up by a portion of the first specialists. One of the critical creators who you should investigate is Dan Kennedy. He has kept in touch with some incredible books throughout the years and is an extraordinary asset for you to utilize.

Ideally, this part on copywriting techniques will help you in improving as a marketing specialist. The key behind successful copywriting is to utilize the equations that have been created while putting your very own turn on what you're composing. Copywriting strategies are significant because individuals have built up these in a specific approach to be successful, which is as it should be. There is no compelling reason to rehash the wheel since this may baffle for you over the long haul as you'll see that you have fewer sales while investing more exertion. By setting aside the effort to pursue working methodology, you'll set yourself up to expand potential sales when building up a sales letter.

Marketing specialists have an exceptionally fascinating specialty with regards to that you can utilize your very own composition to enable you to create leads. If you find that you had many inconsistent advertising methods, consider building up a sales letter to help get qualified leads. If you build up a successful sales letter, you can send this out in amounts which you pre-decide. The magnificence of this is you can evaluate the measure of work that you need to do in a given month and mail out that many sales letters.

After having utilized a reliable sales letter for a specific timeframe, you will recognize what the reaction rate is, and this will enable you to know how much business you ought to possibly get from mailing a particular number of letters. This can ensure that you generally have customers coming into the entryway when you need them to. It can likewise enable you to all the more likely example the business after your life and way of experience with the goal that you can hurry up when you have additional time and back things off when different pieces of your life become busier.

If you have many customers who are telemarketers or you might want to begin creating telemarketers as potential customers, you might need to investigate building up a sales letter for one of these organizations. Telemarketing has turned out to be significantly more costly and increasingly inconsistent nowadays because of new laws, and it is an industry with high turnover. Building up a sales letter to send to qualified prospects to start with can make telemarketing increasingly viable for these organizations and conceivably lessen turnover. If you can measure the reserve funds in training employees just as in better sales, you will end up called upon by many telemarketing organizations since you will have placed yourself in their shoes and can comprehend the business battles that they experience.

The last way that we will utilize a sales letter and one manner by which you could expand your business is to center upon dental specialists and specialists office. Regularly these professionals are reliably searching for new customers, and this could be an approach to enable them to out. You could utilize a sales letter to help stimulate referrals.

Some Power copywriting tips

Here are five of the Motivational Triggers that Make People Buy

1. Individuals need to get more cash-flow. They might need to go into business, find a higher paying line of work, or put resources into the securities exchange. This will make them feel successful.

2. Individuals need to set aside cash. They might need to contribute to the future or put something aside for a significant buy. This will make them have a sense of safety.

3. Individuals need to spare time. They might need to work less and invest energy making the most of life's delights. This will make them feel progressively loose.

4. Individuals need to look better. They might need to shed pounds, tone their body, or improve their facial highlights. This will make them feel increasingly appealing.

5. Individuals need to discover some new information. They might need to figure out how to change their vehicle oil or manufacture a deck. This will make them feel increasingly smart.

How to avoid the most common copywriting mistakes

None of us are flawless. As the familiar axiom goes, even monkeys drop out of trees in some cases. What's more, even an expert copywriter may commit an error every once in a while. Here are a few slip-ups each copywriter has set aside a few minutes or another.

1. Overlooking your audience. When you are copywriting, you are composing it for somebody. That individual might be your customer; in any case, the audience is the individual you need to act depending on what they have perused. It does a whole lot of nothing to write to fulfill a specific customer if the audience doesn't react to what you have composed. Ideally, you have gotten yourself a customer who knows the audience he is endeavoring to reach.

2. Not knowing your item. When you are endeavoring to expound on something that you don't have any acquaintance with, it appears. Nothing is more terrible than finding out about an item when the creator did not recognize what they were discussing! Few out of every odd composition employment can be in your most academic subject field. However, you should set aside the effort to know something about the item you are expounding on.

3. An excess of detail, or not enough. It is once in a while challenging to realize precisely how much detail to expound on. You need to give the audience enough information to catch their eye, however less information that they feel overpowered.

4. You compose excessively. Individuals today don't have a great deal of time to peruse, so if you cannot catch their consideration with your message rapidly, you will miss out on your opportunity. You have to ensure your first words are, and after that, the peruser will remain to perceive what you need to state to them.

5. You don't make it simple for individuals to do what you need them to do. When you need somebody to purchase something from you, you need to make it simple for them to discover the cost of your item and get it. If you need somebody to buy into your pamphlet, you bring to the table them a simple method to buy in, ideally more than one way. If you genuinely need somebody to accomplish something, make it simple for them to do it.

Five Copywriting Mistakes to Avoid

Keep in mind the significance of good copywriting - in case you're starting a substance advertising system, and you'll have to make an accomplishment of it to accomplish the ideal outcomes.

When your substance does not get the point over, you may lose potential deals and harm your organization's notoriety, which is the reason it's essential to put your copywriting effort in steady hands.

The following are five common copywriting botches that must be maintained a strategic distance from:

1. Exhausting features

'The Father of Advertising' David Ogilvy best aggregates up to the significance of the unassuming feature:

"By and large, fivefold the number of individuals read the feature as the body copy. When you have composed your feature, you have burned through eighty pennies out of your dollar."

If your feature is unfit to attract the peruser, that open door for a deal is more likely than not gone.

A feature ought to be snappy, luring and hard-hitting, and fit for attracting the peruser initially.

2. Highlights without the advantage

A component tells the buyer the item's capacity, while the advantage clarifies why they need it.

Great copywriters present the highlights before utilizing them to persuade a potential purchaser of the item's convenience. A buyer will disregard things that don't straightforwardly profit them.

3. Utilizing the equivalent meta title for each web page

A descriptive, informative copy is significant mostly - yet it likewise needs to get saw, which is the place website streamlining (SEO) comes in.

A Meta title uncovers the name of a webpage and is perused via web search tool robots and guests to the website. To seem higher up the rankings, they have to speak to the previous first and the last second.

When the similar Meta title is utilized for each page, your site won't be appropriately upgraded. This may involve its inquiry rankings, and its capacity to illuminate potential customers regarding your business' items and administrations.

4. Saying excessively... or on the other hand close to nothing

A copywriter must comprehend the peruser and the item. Some copy may involve multiple pages of information. However, others may require a single tweet to get the point crosswise over and accomplish the ideal outcomes.

The significant point to recollect is to be compact. Word economy is central - in all respects once in a while can a 3,000-word article not be diminished to 2,500 or 2,000 words. Succinctness keeps unnecessary information from jumbling your copy.

5. Missing the invitation to take action

When you have an 'a snare,' your peruser and potential client requires a delicate push the correct way. Approach them to agree to accept a bulletin, similar to your page on Facebook or tail you on Twitter. If you request a particular activity, the peruser will frequently oblige.

The Top Copywriting Mistakes You Should Avoid Doing Today

Today, content is as yet one of the mainstays of a fruitful web or blog website. If your web or blog website dependably has good substance, you build up yourself as an industry or market pioneer or expert, it helps drive more traffic, and it lifts brand introduction or acknowledgment. It likewise helps pull in more deals.

In that capacity, a ton still depends on proper copywriting methods and systems. When you distribute terrible substance, your believability can be adversely influenced, you mood killer and send guests away, and you accidentally dishearten them from purchasing your items or putting resources into your administrations.

In case you're new to copywriting or confounded regarding why your substance is by all accounts pushing guests away, you might submit some grave mistakes that are harming your web or blog website. The following are the top copywriting mistakes you ought to abstain from doing, starting today:

Thinking of exhausting titles and features. As a publicist, remember that regardless of whether you have the best substance if your claim or feature is awful, nobody is going to tap on or read it. Moreover, another oversight publicists often make attempting to be over-the-top and excessively unique. Even though innovation is an unquestionable requirement, it is additionally vital that you don't go over the edge. You'll finish up confounding and notwithstanding baffling your readers when you think of too preposterous features.

You promise a ton of things. The good substance is something that ought to convince readers to make a move. Nonetheless, encouraging a lot of can have adverse outcomes. Readers today can make sense of when they're being deceived and will leave without delays if your cases are excessively preposterous. Regardless of whether your group of onlookers trusts your cases, these guarantees can be a tremendous disadvantage for you since you will have inconceivable desires to satisfy. When composing the content, dependably speak the truth about what you can offer. You can zest these offers a bit however never go too far that you'll lament doing it.

You are speaking a lot about yourself or your image. A great deal of web and blog locales still have this issue today. The lion's share of the substance is for the most part about materials about themselves, their group, and the organization. As a marketing specialist, you need to comprehend that consumers visit your web or blog website to discover answers or answers for their inquiries and issues, not to find out about you. Ensure that the focal point of the web or blog website ought to be your administrations and what you can offer to your guests or end-clients.

You are stuffing an excessive number of languages in your substance. In conclusion, the regular client won't think about the business language you use. The utilization of such a large number of words can erode a customers' patience and break your transformation rates. A consumer needs to comprehend that you can meet their prerequisites and can help tackle their issues productively. They don't have to realize that you are a virtuoso who knows the intricate details of the business you are in.

Copywriting - The Big Copywriting Mistakes That Could Be Killing Your Sales

Are your copywriting mistakes executing your deals? Indeed, before you can respond to this inquiry, you need to realize what copywriting is. This is known as the way toward composing advertisements and articles that advance an idea, regardless of whether it is an individual or a business. The whole concept behind copywriting is to convince the individual who is understanding it. So since you have a superior comprehension of what copywriting is, you can now unmistakably distinguish any issues that might slaughter your deals. So let's investigate.

The first enormous mistake is the most widely recognized. At whatever point individuals are copywriting, they will in general, spotlight on the business or the promoter. This won't influence anybody to attempt your item or use your administration. You need to consider how the thing will identify with the purchaser, not to the promoter. In this way, you have to concentrate on the buyer, not the developer!

It does make a difference in your identity promoting. Another deadly copywriting mistake is when companies use bad headlines that don't catch the eye of the individual understanding it. This is a significant deals executioner. When your advertisement is beside another organization (that is selling a similar item), and their promotion "hops" out additional, individuals are going to tap on that advertisement. Accordingly, you are slaughtering your deal before you even get an opportunity to make one. Think about your feature as the attempt to seal the deal to get the prospect to peruse the whole advertisement.

The following enormous mistake that individuals are doing when copywriting is that they are assembling an excessive amount of data. The data should be separated into short, discernible arrangements of data. That is the reason it's in every case great to use things like shots to list your data. Individuals don't prefer to peruse, especially on the web, and they usually end up skimming over data. This implies they are not going to read all that you need to state if you don't split it up a tad.

Last, however not the least, you have to realize that copywriting should stream like a typical discussion. It ought not to have a whole bundle of too many great words, because you are only going to lose your client. They have to see that they are purchasing from an individual only like them. Relatively few individuals stroll around and use huge words while they are conversing with their companions. What might you instead purchase from, an advertisement that uses just huge words or a promotion that felt genuine, similar to it originated from the heart. I think the appropriate response is anything but difficult to see!

When your copywriting skills are weak, it might be a smart thought to employ an expert marketing specialist. Having an incredible duplicate is the absolute most crucial factor that will choose if your business will flourish or bomb pitiably.

Simple Copywriting Mistakes to Avoid

Most importantly, you are the leading advertising component that can guarantee your prosperity; no framework is flawless. Web-based advertising isn't immaculate, yet nothing points that out more than when you endeavor to showcase your items or administrations on the Internet. This remains constant for a wide range of internet showcasing efforts and is noteworthy in the field of offers copywriting. We aren't alluding to the standard deformities, but instead genuine copywriting bungles. Blunders that can be effectively revised by permanently sealing your article, or having another person survey it, are incorrectly spelled words, grammatical mistakes, mistaken linguistic structure; these are healthy, apparent mistakes and effectively fixed. Once in a while, these simple issues are not by any means, the only copywriting mistakes that are made. At the point when publicists initially start, many aren't looking for some of the errors that may appear to be simple to us. The duplicate does not do well in deals. We need to keep away from you having your copywriting "lost in interpretation" and have given some broad appeal to you to evade those kinds of mistakes.

The idea of split testing is a significant one in copywriting, and not doing such is one of the greatest mistakes made by marketing specialists. As an extremely effective way of seeing what does and doesn't work, split testing will support you compose fruitful duplicate. Publicists that disregard it, for reasons unknown, won't understand the ideal outcomes since they won't pursue their market. They keep in touch with one form of a business duplicate and put it out, that is about it. This is a risky move, provided that it doesn't work, you've put all your investments tied up in one place. With regards to internet advertising, even the scarcest varieties can cause dramatic differences in change rates. Transformation rate can be improved by activity as straightforward as merely changing the duplicate feature.

Regardless of the numbers, however, there are numerous individuals out there that would prefer to overlook split testing and continue indiscriminately. If you are reluctant to look at which variants of your duplicate item the best outcomes, you are relinquishing any additions that could be accomplished.

Tributes are another critical component to incorporate into your business duplicate. Your potential customer needs some type of affirmation that your item is reliable and worth their buy. They should be persuaded that all that you state is valid. This is the place tributes from your past customers just as different specialists in your specialty can do ponders. Your prospective customer will settle on their buying decision considerably more immediately when they comprehend others have been satisfied with your administrations.

So recollect that copywriting is a craftsmanship that can be enhanced with training and time. When you commit a few errors, gain from them. By following the simple tips above, you will most likely compose duplicate that will enable you to net the best outcomes for your online business.

Copywriting Mistakes You Should Never Make

When you want to compose your very own duplicate, OK be the scarcest piece curious why such a significant number of copywriters bomb wretchedly with their business material? It's difficult to cover every one of the reasons, yet there is one general and huge reason which is neglecting to keep away from specific kinds of errors, which is what we're here to discuss.

A straightforward error that heaps of copywriters make isn't knowing the fundamental subtleties of the item they are selling. When you don't have much learning about the subject, you'll experience serious difficulties endeavoring to persuade the prospect to get it. Your chance would effortlessly peruse you and realize that you don't think a lot about the item. This will negatively affect your transformations just as on your business rate. It is essential to know the issue all around - inside and out information is critical for a marketing specialist. When you have adapted everything to think about the item you can inventively play up its advantages.

When you are secure with these things, you can be completely clear with your composition and ensure that the purchaser gets a rational thought regarding the item. Think about the feature as the business duplicate for your duplicate since that is the activity it needs to do - get your letter read. When you don't have a fascinating feature that catches the eye, you lose deals because very few individuals will peruse past the feature. The marketing specialist possibly has seconds with regards to the function and getting a positive reaction from the peruser. So that is the reason all the professional copywriters invest a great arrangement of energy in the purpose. Some great copywriters will encourage you to utilize the most significant advantage of your item in your feature, you know - hit them over the head with a sled. If you compose an element that functions admirably, at that point, your activity will be a lot simpler.

Additionally, you indeed should be cautious about altering and fixing any syntax or spelling blunders. Your point here is to make deals, not break them by sound unprofessional. You ought to dependably, dependably ensure that you're editing your direct mail advertisement before it goes live before your intended interest group. It's a simple activity, so don't disregard it or overlook it except if your work is continuously impeccable. To ensure you can peruse it a few times while checking for different kinds of blunders. When you stay away from these common slip-ups, you will get a significant decent come back from your copywriting.

A simple technique for writing copy that's easy to read

Most of the individuals have no clue how to compose a proper sales copy, not to mention an offering one. Investigate the internet, and you'll understand. So if there's one bit of leeway, one edge you can increase over your competitors, it's to pick up copywriting techniques that enable you to create executioner sales copy.

In light of that, here are seven copywriting techniques you can execute now and watch your changes take off:

1. Before you do whatever else, you have to realize who you're writing to. Mediocre copywriters will, in general, avoid this altogether because they're excessively fretful. That is a major mix-up. If you know your identity writing to, you can promptly press their problem areas and easily make that deal. To have a little knowledge into who your potential clients are, you use instruments, for example, Quantcast or Alexa to demonstrate to you the socioeconomics of individuals visiting your rival's site.

2. When you get a thought of your identity writing to, the subsequent stage is to make a symbol. A symbol is a projection of yourself. In case you're 20 years of age and you're attempting to offer back torment calm to an older market, it's conspicuous you're not going to be extremely persuading. In case you're 65, you are seen as an increasingly trustworthy source who comprehends their issues. So plan your symbol so that it best identify with individuals who may be keen on your item.

3. With your symbol planned, you would now be able to begin assembling your site. Given your token, you'll have to structure so that in steady with the individual you seem, by all accounts, to be. A youthful hip market may anticipate that your site should have more extravagant accessories with fresh designs. A more traditional market may have slower internet connection since they don't see the need to pay that additional month to month charge, and hence probably won't almost certainly load your site if it's excessively vigorously stacked. Regardless, you ought to dependably seem proficient and ensure your website is anything but difficult to explore.

4. It's just since you should consider your feature. As I would like to think, the general feel of your site (web architecture) could easily compare to your function since it shapes the early introduction. Your feature is additionally essential to the achievement of your website. Once more, an essential element is steady with the craving of your potential client, your symbol, and your web architecture. For instance, a youthful market may specific dialect, while an old market has its own. Regardless, the exemplary "rules" of features apply, guidelines, for example, it must pass on an extraordinary advantage and that it's by and large eye-catching.

5. When perusers achieve your online sales letter, they don't commonly peruse every word you compose. They examine through it, scrutinizing maybe just about 5% of what you composed. Luckily for you, that is uplifting news since that implies you can change over well regardless of whether you can't compose! The significant part is to create the pieces they do peruse compellingly. Bodes well? Those parts are commonly the feature, the initial couple of sentences of the first passage, the sub-features, the P.S, the certification, and the call to action. Each part has its motivation and their copywriting technique you need to ace.

6. Since your perusers filter, you need to make your site simple for them to examine. The best approach to do that is to separate large lumps of words into short passages and use a lot of features to abridge what those short sections are discussing. You ought to likewise utilize an extremely enormous, exceptionally prominent call to action order button since you need individuals who are prepared to purchase to have the option to discover it rapidly.

7. In executing all the work to manufacture your site, never under any circumstance, disregard your objective

peruser. Building an enticing website takes, at any rate, a couple of days or potentially even half a month and it that time, you'll be more likely than not overlook your goal. So review a vital note and glue close to your screen. A sign that says, "Recall your identity writing too!" (Yes, it's that significant.)

So would you be able to perceive what you just accomplished? You accomplished what numerous different copywriters did not - consistency in your sales copy. This copywriting technique is precious if you recognize what you're doing, and it's a vital aspect for creating an enticing sales copy. Consistency and pertinence - rehash that three dozen times, ace them and you're most of the way there on your voyage to be an ace copywriter.

10 Effective Copywriting Techniques

The advanced media age has made a growing demand for copywriters. While this used to be a fringe freelance job about ten years prior, top copywriters would now be able to procure six-number compensations. You need to realize how to pull in perusers. Your articles and blog postings must force stories. A few themes are helpfully appropriate for this purpose, whereas others are tough to work around.

For example, a copywriter who needs to convey a blog for an online the travel industry organization can discover imaginative approaches to pull in buyers (who does not dream of making a trip to outlandish spots with abundant greenery, white sandy shorelines, and turquoise waters?), however a copywriter connected by a bookkeeping firm will commonly have a progressively troublesome time making an exciting account.

The best copywriters are the ones who can make a bookkeeping story sound like a secret novel with turns and sub-plots (OK, perhaps we are a bit excessively emotional. However, you do get the point). Here are ten copywriting techniques for you to take a shot at to improve your copywriting aptitudes and hop up the pecking request in this industry.

1. Research Your Subject

The first of ten copywriting tips is a basic one. You can infrequently write interesting material dependent on the essential information you may have about a subject. The more research you do, the additionally interesting realities and knowledge you can pass on to your peruser.

2. Know the Audience

Another essential guideline that bodes well naturally, so we trust it won't require much persuading. Who is going to peruse the article ought to be one of the first addresses your answer before you begin composing. When the substance is for the general population, you will exhaust them away with gobbledygook, yet it is for copywriters than they will need to know precisely what gobbledygook implies and will find it.

Utilizing language when focusing on experts in a specific field may lead them to be somewhat awed and will turn out to be progressively receptacle to your message.

3. Dazzle with Interesting Headlines

Initial introductions matter. When you make copywriting content, your perusers structure their initial introduction dependent on the title and features of an article. Try not to be hesitant to invest additional energy concocting fun and hypnotizing headings.

4. Portray a Story

There is no better method to begin your substance with a spellbinding story. Even better, leave the finish of the story until the finish of the article, driving your perusers to peruse the whole content to discover how your account closes.

5. Attempt Picture Perfect

You might write, yet that does not mean you have to limit your imaginative aptitudes to the composed word. Make your substance all the more interesting just by making the introduction outwardly engaging. Addition pictures identified with the subject and use headings, passages, and hues to surpass your rivals.

6. Figure out how to Break Rules

Try not to be hesitant to break sentence structure, punctuation, and structure rules. You can't do it all through the content; it will just make you resemble a trick. However, the best copywriters realize how to play with words and standards to make enrapturing expressions and structures.

7. Supplement a Relevant Quote

For reasons unknown, we are altogether captivated by what others need to state, mainly when the expression is originating from a prominent individual. A statement can be displayed in italics, energetic, or focused on a content that is adjusted left. It enables you to make some void area to separate your substance in various parts. You can even begin with a statement to open your content, creating enthusiasm for what is to come. Comments are a flexible device that each copywriter needs to figure out how to consolidate in their content.

Don't go over the edge and put in each article you write. Where pertinent and proper a statement can help change the dreariness of content and make the unknown substance.

8. Differ Your Tone and Lengths

An article where each section or sentence is of an equal length can look very dull, same for the tone. Supplement some vitality in your substance by exchanging the sound and shifting ranges or your sections.

9. Infuse Your Personality

As such, form your image. When you begin composing, you will figure out the kind of tone you like to depict in words. Let this turned into your calling card. It is a fantastic promoting instrument to pull in customers.

10. Have a Short Memory

Composing is craftsmanship! This essential certainty will enable you to traverse extreme occasions. Much the same as a well-known painting that specific individuals may discover ghastly, a portion of your best-composed work will get negative comments. Assess all of the input you understand and apply it at whatever point it uses, yet don't get down on yourself when you believe you have worked admirably, yet the awards don't come to your direction. That is only the idea of this business.

These copywriting techniques are straightforward proposals that can enable you to improve your content. Content prerequisites are continually growing in the online life age. Utilize web-based copywriting administrations to redistribute your work to an online copywriter. You can utilize the previously mentioned copywriting tips to enable you to assess the redistributed work.

Copywriting Techniques All Writers Should Know

Step by step instructions to Create Good Copywriting techniques

As you most likely are aware, there are specific standards for good copywriting. Furthermore, it is significant for you to get them. Just when you realize the fundamentals should you attempt to turn out to be increasingly inventive?

Similarly, as with some other capacity, practice makes for better execution. The more you compose, the better you will write, if you begin by following the necessary standards.

It is anything but difficult to enable messy propensities to crawl into your composition. The exertion you put into the rudiments presently will work well for you later on. There are specific professional copywriting techniques that you necessarily should pursue. If you overlook them, you uncover yourself as a novice, and your endeavors will be dealt with in like manner.

It is not necessarily the case that you can't act naturally or that you can't intentionally disrupt norms. You ought to do this with a reason, not out of numbness. Now and again, you will undoubtedly go past the standards into new skylines of imagination and style. Know the rules first!

You will likewise locate that most composing is direct. It doesn't call for astute developments that regularly don't work. Along these lines, when you clench hand tarting out remain with attempted and tried techniques. Indeed, any composition requests innovativeness. In any case, keeping it straightforward does not mean you are not imaginative.

Keep It Simple

Many starting authors trust they will awe by being as confounded as could be allowed. Not really. Being innovative in your composing does not mean being unpredictable or sounding scholarly. Being basic in your composing does not mean being dull or suggest an absence of astuteness — the less complicated you're copywriting, the better.

The entire thought of composing is to impart. You would prefer not to make your perusers battle. When you form, it implies that a more significant amount of your perusers can comprehend what you are stating. Unquestionably this methodology won't affront your progressively taught or scholarly perusers.

Make Flow In Your Copywriting

Always guarantee your duplicate "streams." Good copywriting likewise concerns setting out what you need to state in a consistent succession. The article should usually stream from one point to the next. Try not to bounce in reverse and advances between thoughts or things of information.

Cover every part of your story entirely and separately before proceeding onward to the following section. It indicates when you have an after-thought and endeavor to cover it with a new paragraph further on.

Utilize short paragraphs. The ideal way to separate your items is as per subjects or thoughts. One thought, one section! In any case, when you have an excessively long article, it is smarter to cut it in a proper spot. Utilize your paragraph breaks to accomplish smooth progress, starting with one idea then onto the next.

Abstain from Using Needless Words

The Oxford English Dictionary characterizes "verbiage" as a bounty of words without the need or much significance. Keep away from unnecessary words - For instance:

- Actually
- It might be expressed.
- It ought to be recorded.

- As you will review
- To get directly to the point.
- For your information
- It is critical to include
- For your information
- It is intriguing to note

Here are some different instances of "verbosity":

- preceding (previously)
- consequent to (after)
- in abundance of (more than)
- with the end goal of (to)
- on the grounds (because)
- as an outcome (because)
- throughout (amid)
- (without)
- except for (aside from)
- in case of (if)

A Checklist Of Copywriting Techniques

I trust you can always cause improvement to any article you to mean to submit to a proofreader. Think about these focuses?

- Have you composed a solid lead to start your peruser's advantage?

- Each story must have a starting, a center, and a completion. Build up a stream to your account.

- Try not to be hesitant to modify. All accounts profit by altering.

- Try not to endeavor to mirror any other person. Act naturally and let your style grow normally. Remember that style is diverse to the right utilization of words.

- Always improve. The less complex you make your composition, the better.

- When you alter your work, ask yourself: Does this fill an urgent need?

- Go to the core of your story. Try not to squander an excessive amount of opportunity approaching your point.

- Set out your story substance in a sensible arrangement. Try not to bounce around with your thoughts.

- Use a lot of paragraphs. Paper and magazine design does not empower large sections of duplicate. Split it up.

- Short sentences are superior to long sentences.

- Utilize true, action words that fit what you are stating.

- Write in the active voice.

- Lean toward the recognizable word to the fantastical.

- Utilize the correct word instead of the dynamic.

- Favor short words to circumvention.

- Try not to be imagined or excessively shrewd.

- Stay away from exaggerations.

- Try not to lecture your peruser. Show them. Use exchange, stories, and episodes. Try not to utilize a long story.

- Get statements to back your story up and make it wake up.

- Try not to depend on modifiers. These have a little spot in good copywriting.

- Try not to deviate from the central matters of your story.

- Try not to be tedious — state what you need to state in the most economical way you can.

- Try not to utilize pointless accentuation.

- Keep yourself out of the story. If you wish to give a sentiment compose a Letter to the Editor.

Why Copywriting Techniques Can Improve Your Articles For Article Marketing

When advertising your business with articles, it's imperative to get individuals to peruse them. The more individuals that read your items, the more individuals will navigate to your site. In any case, what are a few ways to get more individuals to peruse your articles?

You can apply copywriting techniques to the articles themselves to get more individuals to peruse them.

For example, the most significant piece of the article is the title. The title needs to get consideration. If it neglects to get attention, individuals aren't going to peruse the material. Composing the title resembles writing the headline in copywriting.

By figuring out how to compose headlines, you'll figure out how to write unique article titles. To produce titles that get consideration, take a stab at incorporating an advantage in the title. For example, "3 Tips to Boost Sales by 300%" has power. Another copywriting strategy is to apply earnestness to the title.

After the title, you have to compose convincing opening sections. In copywriting, this is known as the lead. Your opening passages need to get the peruser's advantage, and else the person won't peruse further.

A primary way to compose first sections that get consideration is to utilize the issue arrangement system. Record and identify with the issues that the peruser is having. What's more, demonstrate that perusing your article will give the arrangement.

Your peruser might be wary of your thoughts. There are many "masters" out there who give guidance and guarantee to be specialists. In copywriting, skepticism is dealt with by verifying. So you'll need to demonstrate to your perusers that your thoughts are valid.

You can give evidence by utilizing individual precedents, chronicled realities, research, or measurements. An example of overcoming the adversity of somebody applying your thoughts is another right way to give evidence.

Toward the finish of your article is the place you put your asset box. You will likely have individuals navigate to your site. Much the same as in copywriting, you'll need to compose benefits and a suggestion to take action. Show what the peruser will escape visiting your site. And after that advise the peruser to visit your website.

You could likewise incorporate your USP (Unique Selling Proposition) in your asset box. Your rivals are vying for your perusers' consideration as well, so your USP encourages you to emerge and indicates for what reason you're a superior decision.

Other copywriting techniques you'll need to apply are to write in short sentences, write in short passages, and make your article simple to peruse.

So begin by learning one copywriting method and apply it today. Your article will be quickly improved.

Powerful Online Copywriting Techniques

Online copywriting is one of the most generously compensated copywriting occupations on the planet today. Huge companies rely upon this calling to pull in rush hour gridlock to their sites and to expand their deals. For any individual who longs for turning into an online marketing specialist, here are four times tested online copywriting systems that will incapacitate criticism and powerfully induce in the meantime.

Recount to a story. Everyone cherishes a retaining story that catches the feelings. Narrating has dependably been an effective strategy for seasoned online copywriters in making sympathy with prospects. Stories, especially the ones that can identify with the circumstance of readers, can connect with the brain and heart in manners that other selling methods can never achieve.

Good stories allow the publicist to indicate to readers that he comprehends their circumstance, and he has the item or administration that can help take care of their concern. Also, stories allow readers to reach their determination about what is being introduced to them.

Make enthusiasm for the feature. An effective online copywriting can quickly get a peruser's consideration with the entire first line. Cunningly join the item's advantages with power words like certification, phenomenal, demonstrated, excellent, and so on. A page has ten seconds to catch the eye of readers. In that range of time, a marketing specialist needs to utilize dominant eye-catching words to make readers remain and read the remainder of the duplicate. This is a test each publicist needs to confront; it's somewhat hard yet conceivable to deliver.

Toning it down would be best. A duplicate that is too longwinded can confound and exhaust a peruser. When conceivable, a marketing specialist, should utilize visual cues rather than lengthy paragraphs in clarifying an item's advantage. A duplicate written in this arrangement can make perusing much more straightforward and can make a significant focus increasingly discernible.

Make Urgency. Online copywriting is making criticalness. Readers ought to be prompted to make a move in the wake of perusing the duplicate. They should recognize what they will pick up or lose when they don't organization the item. The copy should state something like: "Free enrollment until July" or "For a constrained time just, request now."

Web optimization Copywriting Techniques

Pursue these procedures to wind up brilliant SEO copywriters

Titling

The title of the substance assumes an essential job in SEO. The title ought to be in such a way it wraps up the catchphrase with the goal that it imparts effectively about what the substance brings to the table. The title is the one that catches the consideration of the peruser — 80 % of the general population look at the body of the substance. The title lures them to peruse further.

Body of the substance

Rehashing the focused on keywords to a degree toward the start of the body has any effect. It is simpler for some web search tools to perceive your bit of substance. Likewise, ensure that it isn't rehashed past a specific breaking point.

Subheadings

This is another territory where you can exploit. Directed keywords can likewise be utilized as subheadings. This helps web search tools perceive the pages as well as improves the clients when exploring various pages.

Equivalent words and Correlated Words

A decent composing ought to contain the focused on keywords as well as similar words and related words of the keywords. This is a significant practice since excessive utilization of the keywords can be diminished; however, the setting of the substance still stays unaltered.

Keep the substance exact and careful.

The setting of the substance ought not to waiver at any expense. It is significant that you remember the peruser while composing. He shouldn't be lost part of the way through. The substance should go some way or the other turn around the watchword and still fulfill the peruser at last.

A decent SEO copywriting ought to flawlessly coordinate the watchword and mix into the substance. The peruser at any stage ought not to perceive the reiteration of the catchphrase. This carries a wrong impression to the site all in all. It must be client focused.

Chapter two

Sample headlines, bullet points, and openings

Figuring out how to compose features is pivotal for advertising achievement. Regardless of whether you're writing a feature for your leaflet, a title for your white paper or a headline for your email promoting the effort, you need those first words your prospect peruses to be infectious and charming.

These seven methodologies will make you consider the creative feature alternatives you can use next time you need an eye-catching feature. The precedents (for a dog food called Healthy Paws) following each tip will enable you to see precisely how to apply every system to your composition.

1. Offer to your prospect's feelings. A little pull on the heartstrings is sure to stand out enough to be noticed. Precedent: Is your dog's food hurting his wellbeing?

2. Tailor your message to explicit customer portions. Each customer needs to be one of a kind. By speaking to every customer gathering's interests and affinities, you'll associate on a more profound dimension. Model (directed to wellness buff ladies): You care about your wellbeing - shouldn't something be said about hers?

3. Be the instructor. Individuals are dependably vigilant for valuable, significant data. Offer to give the data they're seeking to. Model: Seven different ways to enable your dog to live more.

4. Pose an inquiry. Open up a discussion with the peruser by asking them a question they'll need the response to. Model: Why do Healthy Paws have dog tails swaying?

5. Make an offer they can't cannot. When you have an extraordinary idea to convey, don't avoid the real issue. Reveal to them forthright what the offer is with a direct, to-the-point message. Precedent: Get your free example of Healthy Paws - today!

6. Offer the news. Prospects are attracted to things that are new and new. If you have another item, or if there is late news identifying with your item, take a stab at consolidating it into your feature. Model: New investigation demonstrates Healthy Paws dogs live more.

7. Make it individual. Individuals love to find out about what you can accomplish for them. Incorporate "you" or "yourself" in the feature to ensure they get this message. Precedent: Help your dog live more

10 Resume Writing Tips To Land You Your Dream Job

Envision yourself sitting in a business' work area with many resumes falling in around your work area against an opening proclaimed by you in your organization.

The number of opening - 1, and the number of candidates - incalculable.

As a business, you must choose the most meriting, reasonable, and skillful applicant. So it is dependent upon the contender to grab the business' attention out of those several resume applications. Accordingly, composing a resume is tied in with comprehending what employers specifically search for in a candidate's application. Along these lines, never wrongly underestimate the significance of a "decent and eye-getting resume."

Presently, a great and ideal resume isn't a purposeful anecdote. Neither makes them anything to do with the elite schools or remarkable work understanding. A blue collar worker may have an excellent CV, while the resume of a white collar proficient may have an ineffectively kept in touch with one. A decent resume is your initial step at the entryway of a great job; you should surely know that it is your agent to business before you arrive. A resume focuses around the nitty-gritty information about a hopeful that is honest, brief, and to the point; not something that is misrepresented or pointlessly long.

There are sure things that a decent and impeccable educational modules vitae has inside its set edges.

1. As a matter of first importance, choose the organization of your resume. Choose whether you need it to be in a practical or ordered configuration.

2. Compose your resume in powerful action words.

3. Feature your aptitudes and destinations. Make it your resume feature.

4. Be specific about your expert foundation. If you are an accomplished individual, notice your residency with past

employers; and in the fact that you are a fresher, characterize your expert capabilities.

5. Characterize your present pay scale. What's more, remember to put down your average compensation.

6. If your CV is focused towards a specific career way or business, at that point, you should know every one of their prerequisites and notice them in your resume all around plainly. Research and understand the characteristics that will demonstrate to be painful to the business and consider how your abilities coordinate those characteristics.

7. Next, be specific to give each moment individual detail. Feature your contact subtleties.

8. Be proficient, concise, brief, and clean — Dodge from being excessively gaudy with your resume plan.

9. Stick to keeping in touch with one-page introductory letter quite far.

10. Last however not the least, make sure to alter and re-alter your resume once you are finished with composing it.

Keep in mind, the target of your resume is to release your achievements and capabilities to the employers' board of trustees. Believe it to be a promotional brochure, a handout showing your authoritative and career aptitudes.

Composing a Powerful Written Targeted Headline

A web-based article, with a great composed targeted headline, won't just improve your web crawler positioning for your actual catchphrase states however will likewise pull in the right sort of guest from the web search tools. The headlines of your substance page must be able to draw in your guests. The tips are as per the following:

1. Pose inquiries:

Your composed headline must be question situated. Your headline must be as a question with the goal that perusers are compelled to ask themselves something. You are creating an impression which an individual won't almost certainly overlook right away. The motivation behind why I am stating this supposes that your headline is in a question structure; at that point, it implies that you are compelling perusers to think. Compose a few instances of question-based headlines for your intended interest group.

For instance:

1. It is safe to say that you are burnt out on your office routine work routine?

2. Would you like to give more opportunities for your family?

The over two questions center the issue, before the intended interest group. You, by and large, make a headline, significantly progressively compelling when an item is presented before the intended interest group instead of giving the arrangement.

2. Bringing curiousness:

You should add an oddity factor to your headline. This will get the peruser guided into finding out about your offer. Utilizing numbers for clarification is likewise considered as a powerful medium for persuading an individual. You can use numbers to suggest more than one motivation to peruse on. For instance, you can apply the accompanying example headlines, which are as per the following:

1. Need to realize three basic approaches to gain free command post pay?

2. Need to realize the two free valuable gifts that you jump on joining the command post pay program?

You can apply the previously mentioned techniques to compose compelling, targeted headlines. You will then not exclusively have the option to improve your web crawler positioning yet will most likely draw in the right sort of guests from the web crawlers as well.

3. Offering an answer for the issue:

Presently, you would then be able to provide a solution to the question that you have quite recently referenced previously. For instance:

- You can win locally established salary and set aside a few minutes for your family and yourself as well.

The over two precedents are for headlines which give answers for the present cash making an issue.

Your headlines ought to be sufficient to have the option to recognize the theme for the substance. Additionally, your principle material should likewise be similarly significant. Some individuals play more thoughtfulness regarding the content of the composed issue. With regards to the headlines, they may not give more significance. You should always remember that headlines are likewise similarly significant.

The Importance of Having Good Web Content - Tips For Creating Effective Content

Web Content Writing Tips

A standout amongst the essential things to recollect when composing content is this: Keep it straightforward and clear. A great many people discover it multiple times harder to peruse message on a computer screen than on paper. Additionally, webpage guests will, in general, skim over Web content, concentrating on features, bold content, and connections. So make sure to design your Web content, so the data is pure for individuals to discover, read, and get it.

Here are some other valuable tips to support you make successful content.

1. Be brief. Cut out new words in sentences, come to the heart of the matter, and express what you have to state rapidly.

2. Be conversational. Try not to utilize entangled words or business language nobody outside your industry will get it. Compose how you talk, so your duplicate will pass on a well disposed of, friendly and confident tone.

3. Write in little pieces. Gathering thoughts by subjects and present them in small, reasonable lumps of data. Keep your sentences as short as could reasonably be expected and change the lengths, so you hold perusers' advantage. At that point include descriptive, bold headings that will make the content more straightforward to check.

4. Give good data. A great many people go online to discover data about their leisure activities, products, or different interests. Try not to squander their time by placing useless, self-serving content on your site. Ensure you give data that is fascinating, yet also, instructive and advancing. (In fact, many search engines won't consider tosting locales into their databases when they need valuable data.)

5. Utilize clear connections. Go past the usual "click here" connect on your Web pages. Take a stab at something like: "Take our demo," "Get an example," or "Order now!" Not just is this additionally captivating, yet it can improve your presentation with search engines.

6. Connection to reciprocal Web locales. Incorporate connects to Web locales that offer beneficial, not

contending data. This won't just profit your site guests. However, it likewise can support your search motor positioning.

7. Keep your content new. Keep the data on your site intriguing and refreshed, so guests will have the motivation to return.

An engaging plan will maneuver individuals into your Web website, yet the content will make them stick and become purchasers. As it were: Pictures tell. However, words sell. That is the reason your content is a standout amongst the most critical components of your Web website.

Sketching out a reasonable technique for your content is the underlying advance to building a Web webpage. In the first place, recognize what you need to achieve with your site, what data it will incorporate, and how the content will be composed.

Your site ought to give data your prospects need to know to purchase from you in addition to data you need them to realize that will persuade them to purchase from you. (This is an important consideration whether you're selling products, administrations or your company image.)

Need-to-know-type content for potential clients may incorporate data about your company, products/administrations, clients, and tributes. Data you need them to know may include work tests, as often as possible posed inquiries, public statements, reports, articles, and other material that can teach them about your business. Furthermore, remember to incorporate a consistent and compelling advertising message that will change over guests into purchasers. Isn't that the essential explanation behind having a Web website?

While your content must take into account site guests, it ought to likewise be deliberately created for the best execution with search engines. So make sure to incorporate the correct catchphrases in your standard content, Meta labels, headings, and so on. The objective is to make your content speaking to site guests AND search motor. If you enhance your content successfully, you can keep a constant flow of free traffic streaming to your Web website.

Tons of templates, examples, and checklists guaranteed to improve your copy

Nowadays, when many individuals need to be effective in their online organizations, maybe just a single thing stays steady. That copy still principles the web. The quality written substance is the final deciding factor, as the well-known adage goes, is as yet seeming to be accurate today. However, numerous individuals are likewise ignoring the significance of useful copy and that they are composing their web copy or sales letters without anyone else's input, regardless of whether they are inadequate with regards to the privilege copywriting abilities to carry out the responsibility. There are two primary ways to fix this; one is to improve your composition capacities and two, to enlist an expert copywriter. We should discuss these alternatives one by one.

The first, improving your copywriting abilities, can be both cheap and costly. How is it so? It may not cost you a lot of cash to be a superior web author if all that you will do is to download and peruse free digital books and instructional exercises on web copywriting. You may likewise read different sites and sites that are devoted to composing excellent copy for the web. The just disadvantage that you can envision from this strategy for learning is that it isn't sorted out. The majority of the data that you are getting are not intended to cooperate solidly like how an entire composition course could be.

Presently if you are happy to pay, there are different composition courses that you can purchase or enlist too, some are requiring a month to month membership. These were made by fruitful copywriters who have effectively composed for some sites of various specialties. You can get a course for direct copy, advertising copy, website improvement or SEO writing, and other composition courses intended for the web. What amount are these courses usually worth? Some can go from a couple of many dollars or as much as two thousand dollars, and that's only the tip of the iceberg. The incredible thing about this is you can examine alone time and everything incorporated into the exercise plan was appropriately composed and intended to enable you to learn well ordered.

There are additionally different ways for you to improve your copywriting aptitudes. Another is by following a format and changing your composition dependent on it. If you can get a form from a famous copywriter, legally obviously, you can without much of a stretch change any structure needs to coordinate that layout. This is a practical approach when you are composing your very own sales letter.

However, the reality remains that not all are authors. Some perhaps better than average journalists; however, if you are expecting to acquire huge dollars from your site, you can't succeed utilizing only a decent copy. What you need is an extraordinary copy the whole distance. What's more, when you recognize that you are not the perfect individual to compose your web copy, at that point, the best alternative for you is to procure an expert copywriter. Regularly, the more encountered a copywriter is, the higher is his or her composition rates. Try not to hold back on redistributing your composing because the nature of the copy can have a significant effect.

So once more, if you need to improve your copywriting abilities, there are free and paid alternatives for you. Also, you ought to be sufficiently modest to acknowledge for yourself if you need another person to do the composition part for you.

Website Copywriting - How to Improve Your Copywriting Skills

Sound copywriting skills are significant in the matter of pitching deals and getting customers. With the appropriate preparation and assurance, you can promptly improve your website copywriting abilities.

Feedback is essential, particularly when you need to remain in the business. You can utilize the accompanying tips to improve your copywriting and its outcomes.

Research is the way to copywriting convincing substance.

Do some examination about the task to get the majority of the data you need. Use web search tools and free gatherings to reveal this material. You should comprehend the item totally, its advantages, nature, favorable circumstances, inconveniences, essential highlights, and attractiveness. You should likewise gather tributes from fulfilled clients to add validity to your substance.

After the item, you can think about the essential thoughts regarding objective consumers. Think about the first gathering of people and the resulting customers that you have to induce that the item is incredible. You ought to understand the various motivating factors of the consumers, including society, character, and financial considerations.

You can utilize enthusiastic triggers in your website copywriting, for example, the dread of misfortune or shortage to drive inspiration at whatever point relevant.

Comprehend the promoting and publicizing channels

Audit significant websites or read the magazines or papers promotions that you intend to contend with to get a vibe on the tone of the general audience. When copywriting a characterized notice, endeavor to take a gander at the distributed advertisements, at that point attempt to pursue the basic principles and after that attempt to take a shot at the factors that will make your promotions emerge from the rest when it is pitched with various promotions of a similar sort.

Make sense of the main reason for your duplicate. It is fundamentally significant that you compose with your favored thoughts in your brain. Your duplicate's primary focus may be to get prospects to visit your press page or sell an item. You ought to incorporate invitations to take action in your copy with the goal that the group of onlookers can get a few opportunities to take activity while perusing your copy. You ought to likewise whole up the main focal points or advantages of the item or administration.

Underline the best bit of leeway in charming headers and go through subtleties to keep your statements, for example, tributes, confirmed outcomes and item execution.

You should duplicate write in the best possible style applicable to the market needs. Talkative or casual copywriting with a race of professionalism can carry out the responsibility of the business you are working with. Compose as though you are up close and personal with the consumer.

Take time far from the duplicate at that point come back to alter your work. Utilize a feedback mechanism, state somebody you trust, to help evaluate the adequacy of the clone, once in a while only changing the title can give duplicate an all the more explicit or essential tone.

Indeed, you can do this with, a sound dimension of website copywriting can be accomplished with a dash of preparation and a little assurance.

Instructions to Improve Your Copywriting Skills By Focusing On The Reader

Copywriting positions extremely high on the rundown of the most productive skills any person in an independent composition business on the web could learn. The explanations behind this are various, and they pretty much all effect changes just like sales. However, it is valuable to comprehend that we as a whole expected to begin off with no learning.

A significant figure that all experts this field all did were to figure out how to viably compose their very own duplicate.

What an ever increasing number of individuals do is begin outsourcing tasks, for example, copywriting. It is essential to perceive what an elegantly composed bit of duplicate resembles, and that is a further valid justification to wind up capable in this exceptionally significant undertaking.

Frequently incredible duplicate gets the essentials right and very little else. For example, a standout amongst the enormous targets is to set up an essential association with the reader. Like this, you will assist your readers with getting increasingly agreeable and permit their retentiveness drop. You can make your reader feel that you two are the main people on the planet. You always should talk like you are speaking with just that individual, and afterward, you address that individual utilizing an individual language. Remember that as a rule, you truly should converse with that individual one on one to build up a relationship of trust.

You can urge your readers to feel like you comprehend them by reacting to the undeniable inquiries you think they will present. The easiest method to have the option to do this is by robust statistical surveying in which you will discover what to discuss in your duplicate. So in your message, answer those inquiries and discussion about worries that are significant. If your duplicate overall is elegantly composed, at that point doing this can significantly affect the reader. In the fact that the remainder of your sales duplicate is deficient with regards to, at that point, the general effect on the reader, will be less significant.

Headlines in any content are so significant it is difficult to exaggerate that reality. That is equally applicable irrespective of whether you are composing sales letters, content headlines, or original blog entries. Your feature needs to stop individuals, make them read it, and afterward maneuver them into your content. You can produce headlines in an assortment of ways utilizing various techniques for specific circumstances. You would prefer not to miss the point, and that implies you should comprehend your market. It is difficult to turn out badly by just giving them a chance to discover, through the feature, what is the most significant and most critical benefit of your item or administration. The angle that any reader of anything you make is keen on knowing is the thing that precisely you will accomplish for them, and what immediate improvement can be picked up.

Benefit bullets are useful copywriting gadgets principally present in sales duplicate. Nothing is keeping you from including them on sites, writes, or even as the content inside showcasing articles. Well-made benefit bullets work to interface the reader's brain by the power of effect when they read them. Incredible shells will have the impact of creating an aching for your item that won't leave. Separating the total content and giving the reader a break in the reading sequence is additionally why bullets are utilized. You in no way, shape, or form need anybody to feel like they are investigating only a muscular mass of dark content that isn't connecting on a particular dimension with them.

Acing copywriting skills isn't such an overwhelming errand as it shows up, as long as you execute a few or the majority of the recommendations that are given above.

4 Straightforward Strategies For Improving Your Copywriting Skills

Copywriting isn't something you can gain from perusing a lot of articles on the web. Great copywriters all have the absolute most crucial ability that an advertiser can have: to have the option to utilize their words to impact others to purchase things. The great copywriters today have all examined composition, influence, showcasing, and brain research widely for quite a long time. You probably won't require out and out sales duplicate in your business at present, however, a fundamental comprehension of copywriting will enable you to out when you're composing your autoresponder messages, for instance, your article asset boxes or even your presentation page duplicate. Here are four necessary procedures for improving your copywriting skills:

1. Relate to your peruser.

The vast majority hit sales pages or presentation pages loaded up with uncertainty and doubt. How is this going to be not quite the same as the last eBook I purchased or downloaded, they'll inquire. They'll have different concerns like whether they'll have room schedule-wise to actualize your procedures or the necessary capital required to contribute to making your techniques work. Regardless of whether you're composing long structure duplicate or only a short little spiel, you should begin off by identifying with your prospect. Tell them that you comprehend the issues they are looking in their business, that you've been there to, and that you can furnish them with arrangements.

2. Recount your story.

The best sales letters recount to great stories. Individuals regularly gripe about the length of sales letters that they run over, yet that is because those sales letters aren't sufficiently fascinating. In case you're selling an Internet showcasing item went for amateurs, recount to the account of how you used to be a learner also and how you made it on the web. In case you're selling a dating item, recount to the tale of how you used to be the most socially cumbersome individual ever who had no desire for getting the young lady (or fellow). You ought to be straightforward when recounting your story. In case you're utilizing a nom de plume, that is the other issue, yet we'll leave that for some additional time. Come clean in your story, however, use the correct psychological hooks and wording to make your story additionally convincing and use the account to lead into the remainder of your duplicate.

3. Make it about them, not you.

It's normal to need to brag about your prosperity on the web. How frequently have we as a whole observed those sales letters with a heap of screenshots showing "proof of income"? Individuals would prefer not to see that - they need to see their very own records loaded up with the money, and they need you to have the option to show them how. It's not what the item has accomplished for you before; it's what the thing can achieve for them once they buy.

4. Give social proof.

When you tell somebody that you're great, they likely will have a hard time believing you. In any case, if an entire pack of individuals back up your case, at that point, that individual will pay heed. Tributes are great for bringing deals to a close. Customary content tributes are okay, however much more dominant than that are sound, and video tributes since prospects can see or hear that it is a genuine individual that is giving the underwriting. You can take it considerably further and rather than tributes, have contextual analyses, which highlights your understudies' outcomes rather than your own.

The most effective method to Improve Your Copywriting

Everyone who composes a copy for anything can generally utilize a fast audit of some essential tips. For the accomplished copywriter, they are just an agenda against which to gauge their composition strategies. For those with less experience, they are a notice of what they ought to do.

Know your group of onlookers.

Regardless of what you are doing, you should know who your objective market or group of onlookers is. Realizing your client is fundamental to any business. This information is essential for you to ensure your tone and approach are fitting before you begin the composition procedure. For instance, how you approach senior citizens will most likely be altogether different from how you address undergrads.

Dispense with geek terms and 50 penny words.

At the point when your composing is brimming with specific terms and dark or over-refined words, it is just difficult to peruse. Utilizing this sort of language regularly creates a negative disposition concerning the peruser. If you are composing for online distribution, the cleaner the copy, the simpler it is to peruse.

Match your language with your peruser.

One of the objectives of copywriting is to create an agreeable discussion with your peruser. Ensure the language you are utilizing is a similar language your peruser employments. If you are composing for money related experts, you should use appropriate bookkeeping and fund terms. If you are writing for movement buffs, ensure you use words that are fitting for that subject.

Try not to utilize long words.

This is one time when "Keep It Simple, Silly" is fitting. Pick short and powerful words. These decisions create a progressively positive effect in the brain of your peruser.

A straightforward sentence is an excellent thing.

Utilizing short, straightforward sentences is one of the basic standards of copywriting. If you use long, complex sentences that contain explicit certainties and numbers, you can confound your peruser. If composting is excessively complex, it leaves you open to the likelihood that your peruser won't understand what you are stating. You can create pointless disarray. The control required to compose more straightforward sentences helps create a copy that is sorted out and creates the ideal impression.

Check your actualities.

Composing copy to be utilized in showcasing regularly implies you should fuse statistical data points. Each word, each reality, each number in your text is significant. Everything must fit together to furnish your peruser with a positive impression of the great or administration you are promoting. Referring to data incorrectly will hurt your picture and validity. Twofold check each reality and figure utilized for exactness.

Don't over-guarantee.

Your peruser or client needs to know the advantages of utilizing your item or administration. It is imperative to give that obviously and genuinely in your copy. Don't over-guarantee or misrepresent. When you guarantee something you can't convey, your believability will be lost.

Be free enough to be innovative.

Copywriting requires a lot of tender loving care. You should likewise be increasing the value of the organic substance. Keep your standpoint new and work in new ideas, styles, and structures that can improve your copy's eye bid.

Edit intensely.

You should verify your copy for language, spelling, and exactness. You may find that looking into your copy once, at that point setting it aside for a brief span and sealing it again will enable you to address any mistakes preceding production. A few experts suggest that your copy be evaluated at least multiple times before its discharge.

Continue learning.

Work on your abilities. Peruse as much as you can about copywriting. Utilize the web to amplify your examination.

If you are resolved and devoted to improving your copywriting when you approach every task as a chance to gain some new useful knowledge, your composition will turn out to be reliably better and progressively unique.

Three Tips For Improving Your Copywriting Skills

When you sell an item, it is a well-known fact that was copywriting skills (or a gifted marketing specialist available) goes far to selling more. We have only a couple of minutes to catch a guest's eye, draw them into our offer, and make the deal. We have to envision their complaints and questions because most will click away to another dealer as opposed to sending you an email to inquire.

It sounds overwhelming. However, it tends to be finished by improving your very own copywriting skills. However, how would you do that?

Here are Your Three Tips:

1. The hypothesis is Important: Getting to know the nuts and bolts and after that applying them to your own business is a significant initial step to figuring out how to sell progressively through your composition. Begin with a copywriting book or course that takes you from the earliest starting point.

2. Study Others: Take a glance at different deals to duplicate that you find convincing or potentially realize that produces great deals results. Duplicate achieving a similar target market to yours is useful, yet GOOD duplicate in any market will give you generally first intimations to what works and what probably won't work.

3. Test Your Own: As you apply what you figure out how to your very own duplicate, track the outcomes. Copywriting isn't a flat out science, and a few procedures could work. Ensure you are trying your duplicate issues to guarantee you're moving in the direction of persistent improvement.

The Importance of Improving Your Writing Skills

There could be numerous reasons that you need to improve your composition skills. It's a smart thought to consider your objectives before you sign up for a course. There are a few rudiments that each author needs.

A comprehension of the English language is essential. The utilization of functional communication and right accentuation enables your perusers to appreciate perusing what you compose, without getting to be occupied. Various online crash courses in English accentuation and syntax are accessible. Some are even free.

Having the option to spell is likewise significant. Microsoft Word and different instruments make that more straightforward for you. If you have a thought of how a word is spelled, Microsoft Word will give recommended spellings when you are erroneous.

A thesaurus and word reference were, at one time, primary instruments for the essayist. Our PCs have everything except replaced those books. When you are a starting author, a thesaurus lists words that are synonymous or have similar implications. Utilizing various words keeps you from getting to be excess or tedious.

When you have the essentials, there are classes structured explicitly for specific objectives. For instance, if you are keen on composing fiction, verse, or diaries, you should need to take an exploratory writing course.

When you need to improve your composition skills since you are keen on turning into a columnist, at that point you need a reporting class. The journalistic style of composing is decidedly not the same as the innovative style.

Journalists have severe principles to pursue. Their utilization of descriptive words and verb modifiers is constrained. Even though things have changed relatively lately, journalists should be impartial, except if the piece is proposed for an article segment.

If you are an entrepreneur, business visionary, or marketer, copywriting may be your objective. Copywriting is utilizing words to urge the peruser to make some move. To improve your composition skills around there, you can take classes or begin perusing promotions or direct mail advertisements.

As a result of web marketing, numerous publicists become familiar with the rudiments of natural website improvement, as well. Site design improvement builds the odds that your duplicate will be perused or that your target market will see the articles that you compose.

Regardless of what sort of things you expect to compose, none of the courses is an exercise in futility. The more you know, and the more that you practice, the more your composition skills will improve.

How to build a powerful sales message that makes money

Deals Messaging - the expressed reasons you offer individuals to purchase from your firm - is the establishment on which every one of your deals and advertising endeavors rests. Unfortunately, most organizations do not have a definition for their business informing, not to mention a strategy for creating and conveying it. The outcomes are a large number of dollars in lost income, higher deals costs, and missed rewards.

Deals informing is the establishment for every one of your sales and showcasing endeavors.

Here is your opportunity to part from the pack and improve your upper hand. Utilize these best ten standards to make a definition for incredible deals informing that will empower your organization to win more requests, increment piece of the overall industry and improve edges.

1. Explicit to One Offering. Deals informing is tied in with offering one offering - a total item or administration. If you sell various items and administrations packaged together, at that point you can think about this as one advertising. If the objects or administrations are sold on a standalone basis, at that point, you should have separate deals informing for each advertising.

2. Focus on Each Buyer. There are various buyer types to consider, including the prospect, customer, channel partner, industry expert, and financial specialist. There are likewise buyer jobs like User, Technical, and Financial. It's crucial to identify buyers by offering, by title, and my career so the business informing resounds with every buyer's advantages and point of view.

3. Answer Buyer's Primary Buying Questions. Every buyer has distinctive purchasing questions. For instance: Prospects are asking, "For what reason should I purchase your answer as opposed to an aggressive choice?" Customers are asking, "For what reason should I continue purchasing from you?" Channel Partners are asking, "For what reason should I disperse your item or administration?" Each buyer's questions are unique, and in this way, require customized answers.

4. Bolster the Product and Sales Cycle. In the beginning times of an item life cycle, the most critical buyer question to answer is "The reason should I change what I as of now do and purchase an item or administration like this?" The problem has nothing to do with your organization. It's tied in with teaching the buyer on why they should roll out an improvement. The essential objective is to make a purchasing occasion.

In the later phases of the item life cycle, when a market request is set up, the essential purchasing question movements to "For what reason should I purchase your answer as opposed to an aggressive alternative?" It's about focused separation and teaching the buyer on why they should purchase your advertising. The essential objective is to request your organization.

Incredible deals informing underpins each period of the business cycle.

Like the item life cycle, the business cycle has particular stages. For instance, suppose you're selling a beginning time item. Toward the start of the business cycle, the essential purchasing question to answer is, "The reason should I meet with you?" Once you have a gathering, the following stage in the business cycle is replying, "For what reason should I change what I as of now do and purchase an item or administration like this?" The last period of the business cycle is then replying, "For what reason should I purchase your answer as opposed to a focused alternative?" Great deals informing underpins each stage in both the item life cycle and deals cycle.

5. Decide the Key Differentiation Factors. There are five essential separation points, including Time, Money, Risk, Strategic, and Personal. The higher amount of these separation points you claim to, the almost certain you are to draw in and make buyers.

6. Apply the Black and White Factor. Various examinations infer that the mind grasps best when given apparent complexity between contrary energies. Explanations like "We are one of the leading..." isn't as convincing as "We are the pioneer in..." Use bunches of pointedly differentiating descriptive words like Only, Fastest, Easiest, Best, and so forth to make incredible deals informing.

7. Test Against the Me Too Factor. To have great deals informing, particularly for aggressive separation, no other organization ought to have the option to make similar cases that you do. The buyer must see that your organization is not the same as the various aggressive choices and merchants.

8. Compose into Three Points. Individuals recall things best when they are displayed in gatherings of three. The mind works this way, to enhance your business, informing for most significant adequacy by fusing this critical rule.

9. Outline on One Page. The response to each purchasing question must be rearranged to a one-page design for a couple of reasons. Your business reps can't recall and well-spoken more than this and your buyers without a doubt won't. To be successful, deals informing must be conveyed to the buyer in edible sums.

10. Give Proof Points. Most buyers consider your business informing to be claimed. To add greater believability to your key points, you should give loads of proof that your cases are valid. The more proof you have, the more credible your circumstances. The best method to approve that your claims and evidence are genuine is to utilize proof points, for example, customer tributes, contextual investigations, and so forth. The second best proof points incorporate outsider organizations like the International Organization for Standardization or Gartner Group, and so forth. The following best proof points are an exhibition or proof-of-idea.

Poor Online Sales? Increase Your Sales Message

Composing incredible duplicate, which gets individuals to do your first target, isn't as hard as some may suspect. Keeping the message clear, brief, and accommodating is a matter of primary importance. When you provide valuable insights and give accurate data concerning the theme of intrigue, they will continue perusing your message.

To remain on track with the message, and do as such as it were, which is drawing in, and intriguing, requires some thinking ahead from the creator. Research your points and catchphrases first, and get accommodating data your peruser will discover vital to them. Individuals like to get familiar with the sorts of things, which demonstrate supportive to them.

Data which they can use to make their lives simpler, get them more cash-flow, or improve their status among friends, is always useful. Focus on your words legitimately at your peruser advantages, and they will happily keep perusing your duplicate. For instance, if you are, you and a member need to make your sales page progressively viable, basically offer the prospect something other than your subsidiary connection.

Compose an inside and out audit, featuring the essential advantages the item or administration will give them. Doing as such will provide the peruser motivation to need to purchase through your connection. You have helped them settle on an educated choice, and do as such in a manner, which requests to their needs. It is powerful to demonstrate consideration for the guest's enthusiasm, as this gives them the motivation to need to purchase from you. Did you realize that over 95% of Web sales pages fail miserably in carrying out the responsibility of making sales?

There is an enormous explanation behind this. Numerous individuals imagine that since they may know the item or administration they are attempting to sell, they are increasingly able to compose the sales duplicate, then an expert marketing specialist. Understanding the intricate details of an item or administration is indispensable to have the option to expound on it. However, this isn't what makes the deal.

90% of what constrains individuals to purchase, can be found inside how the message is introduced. At the point when your sales message focuses on the pursuer's enthusiasm for an amicable way and draws in their passionate intrigue, it ends up certifiable to them. Individuals like to feel as if the sales page was kept in touch with them, as in the manner in which a companion would give a proper declaration about an item.

Give your sales a chance to page message present the advantages unmistakably, without utilizing advertised up cases that enormously harm validity according to the peruser. Maintain a strategic distance from embellishments at all expense. Compose your sales duplicate as if you were addressing a companion, utilizing straightforward yet captivating words. Utilize striking word-picture style writing to upgrade the guest experience.

Keep your writing in a style and voice that individuals can identify with. Try not to confound your peruser by offering to numerous connects to different destinations, as they may pick to go somewhere else, and your deal is lost. By utilizing the insights contained inside this part, you will almost certainly increase your reaction rates from your perusers.

Get your FREE Sales Page assessment. This report will give a nitty-gritty framework to indicate how the duplicate composition on your Sales page can be made considerably more powerful. It will serve you to help reaction and create a lot more sales.

3 Successful Copywriting Tips For Powerful Sales Copy That Dazzles Your Mailing List

Having a tremendous mailing rundown is just a large portion of the clash of a fruitful email promoting effort. When your supporters neglect to peruse your message, and your endeavors are pointless. Many email advertisers invest so much energy concentrating on structure the rundown that they neglect to focus on a quality promoting message, accepting their messages are being perused. It's significant that advertisers understand that a not exactly consummate reaction might be founded on the item's quality; it could in all likelihood be simply the estimation of the message.

Quality copywriting is the way to getting your mailing rundown to peruse your messages and is frequently ignored. Your promoting message begins with the subject line, which ought to propel your endorsers of open at that pointed message and it closes with a message that ought to go past depicting your item or administration - it should construct trust with the peruser. Individuals won't purchase your item or administration except if they're persuaded that you are reliable and that you have their general prosperity at the top of the priority list, so it's significant that your message reflects energy just as honesty.

By following a couple of straightforward copywriting guidelines, you can improve the odds of your email advertising effort's prosperity and construct trust with your mailing list:

Above all else, recollect that your mailing rundown is contained genuine individuals who will make a buy dependent on their thinking, not yours. Each potential client has three alternatives when a purchase is considered - spending his or her cash with your organization, a rival's organization, or to not buy by any stretch of the imagination. For whatever length of time that your advertising message is concentrating explicitly on the requirements of your objective market, you're improving the odds that your mailing rundown will make a buy.

The subject line key to getting your promoting message to your client - if your mailing rundown does not feel constrained to open the email your email showcasing effort will be a failure. The body of the email can have the most potent sales copy conceivable, yet if it's not opened your prospect will never know. The subject line is the initial move towards structure trust, so it's significant that you are not deceiving. Tell your opportunity what they will discover in the body of your email and give an advantage to perusing your message. Individuals don't purchase items, they buy benefits, and if you've done you are showcasing research you comprehend what advantages your mailing rundown is happy to pay for. You can speak to your prospects by using a couple of copywriting strategies, for example, engaging your prospect's feelings, which gets chances into an outlook where they will make a move outside of their typical conduct. Another accommodating strategy to making the ideal subject line is the Secrets procedure, as individuals don't care for being deserted. There is an assortment of other copywriting tips and traps that will enable you to make a quality subject line, which will help improve the odds that your mailing rundown will open your email.

If your subject line is a triumph, at that point, your mailing rundown is currently confronting your message, and the objective is to ensure that prospects perused it. Clients need the fundamental truth about an item or administration, how it can improve some part of their lives or business and measure quality dependent on the sales introduction as opposed to the thing itself. The main line of your message will decide if the individuals from your mailing rundown will keep on perusing your message or basically erase the email and proceed onward. The first line of your message ought to come to the heart of the matter as it give an advantage that forces your client to keep perusing. Recollect that; you're not by any means the only email advertiser on the Internet, so it's sheltered to accept that the individuals from your mailing rundown have a limited ability to focus - come to the heart of the matter rapidly. As the message continues, it's essential that you convey precisely what the subject line guaranteed, if the copy is off point, at that point you've lost the trust of your peruser and they will proceed onward. The present Internet surfer is eager for data, so attempt to give data that trains them something with the goal that it shows up you're an expert on the point and somebody they can trust. Your mailing rundown must feel as though you're addressing them straightforwardly if your message does not mirror your eager character the odds of getting the ideal activity is thin.

To put it plainly, recollect that your mailing rundown is included genuine individuals and that they are potential long haul clients. Fruitful email advertisers are innovative people, and imagination begins with not just thorough knowledge about your item or administration; it's additionally essential that you comprehend your objective market. Fruitful email advertisers make the important strides towards structure a mailing rundown loaded up with the ideal clients for his item or administration and after that focuses on the advantages. Keep in mind that you're promoting to your review of prospects and that you're addressing somebody that isn't just qualified yet fit for purchasing.

Chapter three

Secrets of headlines that all but force prospects to read your message

Are headlines and titles significant? Most partners, unfortunately, don't understand precisely how substantial headlines and titles are. This ought not to be an offshoot showcasing mystery. It ought to in actuality be pretty obvious.

For instance, when you are on the web assaulted by such a significant number of various titles and headlines "shouting out" to be clicked, what do you generally finish up doing? The appropriate response is pretty basic. You will snap at the most exciting stuff you see.

What this means online is a member who is either a complete disappointment or an absolute achievement. The active associate is the person who thinks of solid and alluring headlines and titles that people can barely stand up to...

This implies you can change the fortunes of your subsidiary program by seriously investigating the headlines and titles that you generally used to get traffic to your partner program site. You have to inquire as to whether the expressions and sentences you use in huge intense are the caring that get a prospect by the scruff of their neck and power them to navigate to your site, regardless of how bustling they are. When your headlines don't do this, at that point it implies that you have recognized one fundamental shortcoming in your offshoot advertising.

To make the sort of titles that will get a large gathering of people of your focused on prospects running into your partner site, you need a profound comprehension of human instinct. For instance, people are necessarily exceptionally childish, hoping to fulfill their very own needs and needs. Furthermore, for the most part, people will react considerably more rapidly to take care of an issue as opposed to anticipating one. In this way, headlines try to tackle problems instead of to counteract them will finish up being considerably more powerful and will unquestionably get gigantic focused on reaction.

One fundamental error with headlines is that when a feature condenses the article so well that one doesn't have to go to the report since they comprehend what it is about. Indeed, as opposed to disclosing to everything, if you can discover a method for causing interest with your feature or title, it will result in general work great.

Utilizing these couple of hot feature tips, you can look again at the headlines that you more often than not depend on to destroy in rush hour gridlock to your member site or blog or much increasingly significant, your partner deals page. Keep in mind that even a slight improvement will majorly affect your subsidiary deals.

Continuously Use Headlines to Grab Readers' Attentions

Headlines have been demonstrated to grab a peruser's attention. These are the main things your prospects are going to take a gander at when they visit your site. Your feature fills in as a smaller than usual promotion to give your chances thought of what your site is about, particularly in importance to your direct mail advertisement.

The three duties of a Headline

1. A Headline Should Announce Your Products' Biggest Benefit

Unless you pull in the peruser's attention front and center, you can rely on your guests to quit perusing in around 3 seconds or less. That is pretty much all the time your feature needs to have any effect. That is the reason your function must grab the peruser's attention by plainly expressing the most significant benefit somebody will get from perusing the remainder of your direct mail advertisement immediately.

2. A Headline Should Be Powerful Enough To Make Them Want To Read More

Your feature ought to propel your prospect to continue perusing the remainder of your direct mail advertisement in your site. It is unquestionably essential to own a ground-breaking expression about your feature without giving ceaselessly so much data that somebody won't need to peruse the remainder of the message to find out additional.

3. A Headline Should Deliver An Entire Mini-Sales Message

Looking at the situation objectively, you'll see that your feature is extremely an independent deals message. It is intended to pitch somebody on needing to peruse the body of the word. Readership studies demonstrate that 80% of your prospects will examine just the feature before choosing whether or not they need to know more.

The hardest piece of composing a feature is making sense of what it is you need to state.

Saying the wrong things with the right words means NO SALE!

You have to pass on your point in as few words as could be allowed (to be brief) and not stress if your secondary school English instructor will review your paper. Your objective isn't to demonstrate the world what a skilled and persuasive essayist you are. You will probably make the money register ring! So don't begin concentrating on "how" you are going to state something, start focus on "what" it is you need to pass on to the readers.

Continuously give your feature the regard that it merits. It is the most critical component of your direct mail advertisement. It is the one possibility you need to grab the attention of your crowd. When your feature neglects to carry out its responsibility appropriately, the rest of the parts of the direct mail advertisement will never get their opportunity to excel.

To compose a ground-breaking feature, you need to venture out of your shoes, and instead wear the shoes of your planned client. You need to realize which words will energize them and which ones will put them off to rest.

Most importantly, you need to realize how to utilize those words to make it unimaginable for them NOT to need to peruse the rest of the direct mail advertisement.

Eight Types of Headlines You Can Use:

1. The most effective method to Headlines - People love to realize how to get things done. Such feature dependably stands out enough to be noticed. Indeed, they're presumably the two most dominant words you can use in a function.

2. Privileged insights of Headlines - People dependably need to know "insider mysteries." We want to know things that other individuals aren't aware of. Information is control, and the individuals who have it feel ground-breaking. The majority of us appreciate a decent puzzle, particularly at last when the "mystery" is uncovered.

3. Cautioning Headlines - Remember that individuals are persuaded by the dread of losing something more than the guarantee of increase. "Warning" demands attention and when joined with something relevant to the peruser, is an incredible feature.

4. News Headlines - This tells your prospect something he didn't know previously.

5. Guarantee Headlines - you promise something if the prospect pursues your recommendation.

6. Selective Headlines - Headlines that limit you to a private gathering of prospects. Alert, this sort of feature can dispose of potential clients. Utilize the particular feature system cautiously.

7. Interest Headlines - the reason for this feature is to excite the prospect's advantage enough to make him read your letter.

8. Request Headlines - Watch out for this one as the vast majority oppose being pushed. Utilize less prominent words to improve requesting headlines.

10 Secrets For Perfect Headlines

Copywriting Tips to Help You Master the Art of the Pitch

Composing excellent duplicate takes practice and order, yet it likewise takes something that causes a considerable lot of us to recoil: homework. To compose a convincing promotion duplicate, you will need to take a gander at the task from each edge. Who are you writing for? What would they like to peruse? What is going to catch their eye? What are the best watchwords to incorporate? Would it be advisable for you to utilize a natural, conversational tone, or is this group of onlookers carefully business? The fruitful marketing specialist knows the responses to these inquiries before the person composes even a single word.

When the procedure has started, each copywriting task should begin a similar way: with a headline. We can't pressure how significant the headline is - the achievement or disappointment of your copywriting administrations relies upon your capacity to create a caption with a gravity well that could be estimated by NASA. Hyperbolic as it might sound, if your peruser doesn't make it past the headline, you don't have a peruse. How about we investigate a portion of the mystery systems that you can utilize when copywriting to make a great headline that will work like a magnet for your perusers.

1. Size Matters! It appears as though we start each copywriting guide with this tip, yet it bears rehashing. If your headline doesn't fit conveniently into a Tweet with space for connections and hashtags, it is anything but a fruitful headline. 90-120 characters are the sweet spot and recall that web indexes record the first 65 characters, so ensure that your headline starts with a blast.

2. Maintain a strategic distance from Ambiguity. Your peruser should comprehend what they're getting into before they click your article. If you've unearthed a magnificent quip or bit of pleasantry that might be cunning and eye-getting, however, isn't so clear with regards to the substance of your post, spare it for the subhead or body content. Be smart and talented later - the headline is only the snare.

3. Who Else Wants It? This is one mystery that has been demonstrated to work again and again, and is one of the crucial privileged insights of ethical headline-making: think carefully to infer that your subject is as of now something that others know, use, appreciate, or are generally captivating in, and consequently that your peruser is passing up something significant by not clicking. "Who Else Wants to Lose 10 Pounds?" Well, I positively do!

4. Include a Little Mystery. Utilization of words like "Mystery" or "Little-Known Facts" will help attract perusers, as they will accept they're getting data that others aren't mindful of. "Purchasing a House" is certifiably not a convincing headline - yet "The Secret to Getting the Best Mortgage Rate" or "Little-Known Facts about Getting Approved for a Home Loan," then again, will attract perusers who are searching for bits of knowledge they can't discover anyplace else. Not persuaded that it works? Take a gander at the headline for this section once again. Convinced yet?

5. Use Numbers. By and by, we've utilized this methodology in this very part. Numbers help to evaluate what you're discussing. "Showing signs of improvement Body" is a great headline, however, "Improving Body in 2 Weeks" is better, and "10 Steps to Get a Better Body in 2 Weeks" is even better. With numbers, especially those 10 and beneath, perusers feel like they recognize what they're getting into. An article on weight reduction is as yet an article, and the present Internet peruser is whimsical and needs data in a rush. Ten tips, then again, sounds simple to scale and necessary, and even the most-capricious peruser can stick around for a rundown of 10 things. Second, including the "in about fourteen days" to the end intensifies your case and causes you to emerge in a field of different articles about comparable subjects.

6. Stay faithful to Your Commitments. Since we're looking at making active cases, it's essential to take note of that copywriting doesn't mean hyperbolizing, extending reality, or lying. Ensure that the substance of your post will convey on the guarantees you make in your headline.

7. The Speedy Approach. As we've stated, perusers are flighty. Utilizing the Internet to discover answers and tackle issues have turned out to be second nature to the more significant part of us. Sites offer snappy responses to for all intents and purposes any of our inquiries, from home improvement to human services, and great copywriting takes advantage of this attitude. When you compose a headline that fills the convenient solution, moment satisfaction need, you will be nectar for the rapid honey bee peruser. Things like "Dispose of Carpenter Ants Once and for All" or "The Quickest Way to Get Over a Cold" are nearly ensured to beat articles with similar data with a mellow headline.

8. Enhance It. Thus, you have a decent snare, and you have a proper headline: "10 Ways to Get Rich." Not awful. However, there's some space to develop, and we would amp be able to up your copywriting a bit with the utilization of some incredible descriptive words and hard cases. If "10 Ways to Get Rich" is a decent headline, "10 Ways to Get Filthy Rich in Just One Year" is an awesome one. Keep in mind the other copywriting rules, however;

keep it Tweetable, and don't make guarantees in your headline that you can't stay in your post.

9. Records Always Work. Rehash after me: Lists dependably work. This gets into two things we've just examined - utilizing numbers and stressing rapid perusing. Nobody needs to click a snappy headline to locate a profound mass of content - visual cues, top-ten records, and other evaluated, point-by-point clarifications will dependably be more fruitful than articles with a similar data displayed in passage structure. Copywriting is tied in with catching the skimmers and speed-perusers as they blast through the Web. Other than - records are simpler to compose, as well!

10. Write in NOW. At long last, it doesn't make a difference in case you're expounding on something that happened two months prior; make a point to dependably write-in current state. "Our Company has cast a ballot the #1 organization in our state" sounds okay, however, "Our Company is glad to be cast a ballot the #1 organization in our state" sounds far superior.

The Headline - The Secret Password Into Your Customer's Mind?

Suppose somebody gave you the location of a secret club. The club held inside several eager customers, all prepared to discover progressively about your item or administration. Also, you know everything you have to know to get these individuals to buy from you. Sounds pretty delightful, isn't that right?

Oh, dear, there's one issue. You're not inside the club. What's more, the bouncer at the entryway takes a gander at you and asks, "What's the secret password?" How would you discover a route in so you can do something amazing?

Your feature is the secret password.

It doesn't make a difference how much data you have. It doesn't make a difference in how extraordinary your item or administration. Regardless of whether you knew everything about each, it would not affect. None of it implies anything if you can't get into the club in any case.

128

The equivalent goes for your item or administration. You could have the best offering since cut bread (that's right, I said it.) But nobody would mind if you couldn't get the person in question to stop and pay heed.

This is the reason your feature is so significant. It's the secret password into the brain of your potential client. When your feature neglects to draw in consideration of your target, everything else you compose is unimportant.

Is your feature extremely that significant?

Try not to think you need a feature? Imagine a scenario where you expelled the features from magazines at the newspaper kiosk. How might you realize which to peruse? (Although I'm sure there's one segment of magazines that would at present do pretty well, perhaps far better without the features. That is an entire diverse exchange.

Investigate. Features are all over the place. They're all endeavoring to stand out enough to be noticed. fI you don't have one, your client sees no motivation to peruse on to perceive what you're putting forth. So what occurs?

See you! They proceed onward. Your feature needs to connect with your potential client. At that point be their visit manual to demonstrate to them what they're getting into.

How about we investigate a few precedents

Here are only a couple of instances of the various sorts of features:

1. The News Headline

Is there something newsworthy about your item, administration or business? There is you can include it in your feature.

For example, New Dance Company Changes the Way You Experience Dance.

2. The How-to Headline

This kind of feature guarantees the peruser sound exhortation, data, and the answer for an issue.

For example, The most effective method to Use Overload-Underload Training to Increase the Power of Your Swing.

3. The Question-Based Headline

When you pose an inquiry, the peruser's mind gets disturbed and needs to know more.

For example, Do You Know These Secrets to Surviving College Dorm-Life?

May I show you to your table?

When your feature connects with your group of onlookers, livens their advantage and makes them need to adopt more, you've made sense of the secret password into their brain.

Does your site have a feature that connects with your target gathering of people? Or on the other hand, does it merely state "Welcome" or not have a feature by any stretch of the imagination? Investigate and check whether you can make sense of the secret password. At that point, you can sit down at the table. It's an excellent opportunity to do something amazing.

Easy shortcuts to creating profitable bullet points

Building your very own sales minisites can be somewhat of a task - no uncertainty! In the wake of making an item, you need a site to offer it from, yet for some, this step has a lofty expectation to absorb information. The way toward making a sales minisite is one territory that occasionally prevents potential internet advertisers from benefitting on the web.

This step is essential; you need to profit on the web. You additionally require a sales website to attract affiliates, get engaged with joint ventures, or to give your internet promoting business any believability. It's undeniable; however, why this step causes many web showcasing learners to stop in their tracks. There are a few different ways around this sticking point.

Here are 5 top ways you can quickly use to accelerate the way toward making a first sales webpage for your next internet advertising venture.

1. Use Video.

A video sales page usually has a video, a couple of visual cues, and a purchasing join. When you have shot your sales video at that point, making the page is the simple part. By utilizing video, you promptly get rid of the vast majority of the issues of web graphics, designing content, creating a sales letter, and bunches of HTML coding.

The massive advantage of including video as your sales message is that you can likewise exhibit your item directly there on the screen. This is ground-breaking advertising.

2. Use Outsourcing.

When you choose to re-appropriate your minisite creation, you will require a spending limit to pay your consultant. Fortunately, there are a great many highly talented and innovative web engineers out there who can enable you to out. Independent locales like elance.com or peopleperhour.com have arrangements of the individuals who can make your minisite.

On many of these independent locales, you don't have to pay anything until you are happy with the outcome. Additionally, those keen on taking your venture will show the amount they are eager to take to finish it, so they attempt to "out offer" one another. These two elements will, in general, minimize the expenses and find you an extraordinary line of work at an incredible cost.

3. Use Someone Else's Site.

If you don't have an item yet, you can utilize another person's site and sell their thing as a member. Even though this doesn't get your site ready for action, it allows you to acquire cash, gain involvement, and to fabricate your very own rundown purchasers. This likewise encourages you to learn a touch of breathing space while you get your items ready for action.

Another enormous preferred position of this procedure is that you can see the kind of sites that are changing over guests to purchasers and profits. This can give you great pointers to what you have to incorporate into your very own minisite venture.

4. Use Templates.

Templates are site page spaces. They have every one of the highlights of the finished page like features, subheads, tribute boxes, shot records, and purchasing joins, yet none of the nitty-gritty substance. This leaves you allowed to connect your data and change the template into your own sales page.

The massive bit of leeway here is that your sales page will be your own. Indeed, even-even though you began off with a standard template, your very personal data will transform it into a sales minisite that nobody else has. You can also incorporate your very own graphics, video, and so on to change it into something exceptional.

5. Use PLR Products.

Personal name rights items (or PLR for short) regularly accompany their very own sales destinations. You can ordinarily alter both the PLR item, and the sales site, thus produce an exceptional piece, yet also a remarkable sales minisite. You don't need to do this. At any rate, you should embed your purchasing join into the sales page to make the site your own.

Any of these techniques can cut off the procedure of making your very own high benefit sales minisite. You have to recall that the way toward making website pages is vital to internet promoting, however, to get ready for action you don't have to put in a long time sweating over a hot console.

The First Steps To Building A Profitable List

When you need to be effective, you should do all that you can to achieve that objective. You can't sit before your PC with no thought of what to do, complaining of not getting the benefits you want. You have to work by contributing ample opportunity, cash, and exertion if you anticipate results.

How would you begin?

You should initially pick a specialty and afterward drill down to a profitable subspecialty. This should be possible by first choosing what hobby you need to assemble your business around. This could be something you are enthusiastic about, something you are keen on, or something you need to find out additional. Try not to discount a specialty since you know nothing about it as you will learn as you research and assemble your business.

Nonetheless, don't pick a specialty since it is profitable as you will before long think that it is repetitive to assemble a business around something you have no enthusiasm at all in. You should constrain yourself to make items, compose articles, and market that business.

Squeeze Page Secrets of Successful Profitable Affiliate Marketers

Numerous successful affiliate marketers have been utilizing the squeeze page as their first presentation page to develop their business. This model of point of arrival works very well as it will empower you to gather the guests' subtleties, and you will have the chance to catch up with them through email. Since you will contribute a great deal of your time and exertion in driving consistent traffic back to your site, you will need to ensure that your squeeze page changes over. Here are the following segments you should know:

Part #1 - Attention Grabbing Headline

This is the first segment that your guests will see when they visit your site. You will need to ensure that you put in the most significant advantage in your feature with the goal that it will catch the guests subtleties. When you are merely beginning, you will need to pick one great feature and track the reaction of your squeeze head. When you have a logical progression of traffic back to your site, you will need to test with another feature to attempt and improve the change. The best thing you need to do is to gather your very own rundown of feature formats so you will almost certainly use it at whatever point you need to change the feature.

Part #2 - Bullet Points

You will need to rundown down the qualities that they will get from you if they join your bulletin. This is critical as you will need to guarantee that your newsletters will take care of a portion of their issues with the goal that it will urge more guests to join your rundown. You will need to outline down in any event 3 to 5 benefits in visual cue group with the goal that they will almost certainly look rapidly and settle on the choice on whether they should join your rundown.

Part #3 - Ensure the Opt-In Form Is Above the Fold

The majority of the guests have limited capacity to focus so you will need to ensure that they will probably observe your excellent advice without looking down the site. You will need to make the selection in the procedure for your guests to be as necessary as could reasonably be expected.

Do guarantee that you have put in specific sentences which will let them know precisely the things that your guests need to do to join your pamphlet.

Here are 3 of the many secrets you have to know whether you need to make a squeeze page that changes over more guests into endorsers. Do make sure to continue tweaking your squeeze page so you will get the best picks in changes.

Stories that boost sales--how to write them, step-by-step

The "A" story is the similarity. Once, I saw a direct mail advertisement from Armand Morin where he clarified the power behind a tidal wave... a 600-foot tsunami... it continues building and building then he lead into the viral nature of the program he was advancing. To recount a relationship story, you should start discussing some random fact and interface that to a selling point, similar to I just clarified with Armand's direct mail advertisement.

A simple method to discover random data to kickstart similarity direct mail advertisements is to look for "Snapple incidental data." You can find a rundown of random data, for example, "The city of Los Angeles has multiple times a bigger number of autos than individuals" or "Elephants just rest two hours every day." Pretend you were pitching an item about how to rest better in less time. You could state, elephants sleep two hours out of each day, so for what reason would you say you are spending multiple times that?

A simple story strategy is the Testimonial direct mail advertisement. Get individuals to survey your item, take the best tribute, and transform their primary concern into a headline, their auxiliary point into a subheadline, etc. You can even alter their content and develop a portion of their focuses, with their permission. You can return and meeting that client to get more subtleties. I heard once that giving verification in tributes makes three strides: Convince the prospect that you achieved something, persuade the possibility that another person realized something, lastly influence the chance that they can achieve a similar outcome.

Those are two best storytelling methods for copywriting: the similarity and the tribute. Consolidate them with other storytelling methods I have clarified already, and you have the "W.H.A.T." framework: What-If, How-To, Analogy, and Testimonial procedures for copywriting.

Step by step instructions to Write A Good Call-To-Action

An excellent suggestion to take action is essential to your prosperity on the web. Not at all like the way multinationals run their promoting effort in the disconnected business world, there is no solid invitation to take action present. An entrepreneur has an alternate promoting outlook. Getting prospects to make a move right presently is your goal. In this section, I need to tell you the best way to compose a unique invitation to take action that conveys moment results.

Pose Emotional Inquiries

There is nothing that persuades individuals into making the move you need them to like enthusiastic inquiries. Regardless of the sort of activity, you need them to take, ask them and include cordiality. For example, if you are offering a digital book on the best way to recover your ex, you can pose inquiries like: "how would you feel remaining alone in the room without your stunning sweetheart." Questions go before answer, mainly when you are focused on the right sort of prospects who need solutions to their issues.

Include What's In It For Me (WIIFM)

No one truly thinks about your incredible product if it's comprised of your examples of overcoming adversity. Prospects need a purpose behind making any move you require. After you have inquired about your specialty completely, observe the issues individuals are having, and use it as a WIIFM to support your actual visitor clicking percentage. When a product or an offer does not take care of the necessities of a prospect, there is no compelling reason to select in or click the request catch.

Include Honest Testimonials

Before individuals settle on the choice to purchase a product, they need to realize what number of clients have examples of overcoming adversity. If you sell your very own product, include honest testimonials from your ongoing clients. This would persuade your prospects to see through your product and make a move in making buys. A few times, I have bought a product because I saw some trustworthy web advertisers giving their glow testimonials. If that product helped them, there is nobody it can't do likewise for me. Honest testimonials encourage in your suggestion to take action.

Use White Background

Utilizing a white foundation is a much-disregarded part of boosting your invitation to take action. It's as significant as including a tribute on your site. White foundation with dark content pulls into consideration more than a hued foundation with white or hued content. If your guests have issues perusing your duplicate, making a move has been crushed as of now. Regardless of how much compelling your copy is and the advantages your products give, make it evident by putting these on a white foundation. As healthy as this may be, it can prompt more deals and actual visitor clicking percentage.

Include Money Back Guarantee

If you confide in your product, why not offer an unconditional promise. This could support your transformation rate as individuals would be satisfied to make a move with less influence. All fruitful product owners have a guarantee on their business pages, and it works if you do it well. You can likewise express that you'll enable your clients to keep the product just as recover their cash inside a set timeframe. This is a massive motivation if you ask me, and it will eventually support your deals.

Step by step instructions to Write Great Sales Copy That Sells

One of the most significant obstacles to entrepreneurs, who need to work together on the web, or to support their certifiable sales with a site, is that they don't have direct contact with their customers. Where they would, in reality, have the option to 'sell' their customers on their items, with regards to online business, the procedure is predominantly determined by the customer, who can leave your webpage whenever.

The appropriate response is sales copy; however, what is it, precisely, and in what capacity can entrepreneurs ensure that their sales copy goes guests to their site into paying customers.

It might shock you that composition excellent sales copy is less about hard selling, and progressively about knowing who your crowd is, and what they need, and about structure a relationship where they trust that you are the individual who can offer it to them.

The initial step is to have some thought of your identity composing sales copy for. When you have a site that is quite certain and focused on individuals that have a particular intrigue, at that point that ought not to be excessively hard, in any case, imagine a scenario in which you have a site that could be visited by anybody. Your initial step ought to be to take a gander at your site insights. Most administrations, similar to Google's Analytics, will give you some thought of where your guests are from, which is an excellent begin. Administrations like Alexa.com will make this one-stride further, revealing to you what the average age of your clients is, just as their sexual orientation and other data. That is a decent beginning stage when composing sales copy because diverse age gatherings and sexes will have various needs and wants.

The following stage is an enticing feature. When your landing page still says: 'Welcome to my landing page,' at that point your copy unquestionably needs an update! My site's feature clarifies precisely what I will give individuals who visit my page, and that is the thing that you should go for - a feature that advises individuals what's in store, and gets them energized!

Excellent sales copy additionally invests a little energy promoting your accreditations. It will disclose to your guests what you do, how you have turned into a specialist, and how you expect to impart that information to other people. You could include your certifications or a personal story, and you may find that adding testimonials from your customers additionally goes far to build up your identity, and why your guests should focus on what you state on your site. It ought to likewise give them the feeling that they know you. However - everybody is bound to purchase from an individual or organization that they know and trust, are not they.

A certification can likewise do some incredible things for your sales copy. Realizing that you are eager to stake your profit on your consumer loyalties is an astonishing helper, and it consoles your guests that if they are not by any stretch of the imagination glad, they can at present alter their perspectives later on.

Another significant contrast between excellent sales copy that sells is that it centers around advantages, instead of highlights. Think about the distinction between an element - a vehicle that is light on fuel, and a power - getting a good deal on running expenses. They are something very similar, yet the second description makes it increasingly personal for the individual who is thinking about purchasing that vehicle, and when it ends up private, you are unmistakably bound to make a deal.

The composition, designing, and format of your sales copy are significant as well. Keep in mind that when individuals read on the web, they will in general output more than reading intently as they would in print media. This is the place bulleted records, subheadings, and different strategies for separating the content into a simple to sweep arrangement does some fantastic things. Your guests will almost certainly read your sales copy rapidly, and discover the data that interests them, or that they are searching for snappier and simpler. That is bound to make them read your copy all the more intently, and it's well worth remembering.

The last part of the excellent sales copy is the invitation to take action. When your copy has carried out, its responsibility, your peruser has achieved its finish and is excited for what you're stating, or the item or administration you're selling. The individual in question ought to be prepared to settle on a buying choice, yet if you don't request that to occur, or give the methods, it can't! A few people even add a feeling of direness to their sales copy by advising their peruser that there is a period limit on the offer. This is another excellent method to ensure your sales copy works, however, recall - the key is to get them intrigued, get them to confide in you, and get them to peruse as far as possible when you need to make a deal!

Excellent sales copy works similarly that your sales group does. It tells your customers what you are putting forth them and how it will profit them. It encourages them to confide in you, and it shares data. The actual sales part of your copy typically occurs towards the finish of the piece, not in the first passage!

When your sales copy is elegantly composed, and connects well with the peruser, at that point, it can dramatically affect your sales. Regardless of whether it is expanding the number of calls your real business gets or improving the sales of your online business.

Why not look again at your very own sales copy. Is it composed given your client, or does it bounce appropriately to the hard sell? If it does, it might be the ideal opportunity for you to reexamine your technique, and give your sales copy a facelift. You would be astonished at what a couple of changes can do!

Chapter four

Insider secrets for "amping up" the emotional power of your copy

Like a great many people that have begun as a consultant, I have committed a couple of errors. The thing that matters is, I've additionally figured out how to keep up a lifestyle that the vast majority envy... having the option to rest in, take my little girl to the pool, leave my PC and have two days off in the week... compose and advertise in 'grabs' of time.

Presently I'm not saying I'm winning a full-time equal pay yet, yet considering the measure of time I spend doing it, it pays great. As an intermediate copywriter with two-three years experience, I charge out at A$65 every hour for copywriting, and $50 every hour for promotion the board. It is subsidence, and I charge what my clients can pay... there's nothing to prevent you from acquiring $110 every hour or considerably more down the track.

How far you go with outsourcing relies upon your measure of work hours, rivals in your field, how experienced you are, and how great you are at offering yourself.

Do I need Qualifications and Experience?

For copywriting, capabilities are not required. If you need to compose for a private company, it's likewise obviously better to have worked IN an independent company than to have a publicizing organization/PR foundation. Since self-employed venture individuals don't have the sizeable publicizing spending plan of corporate clients, if you can comprehend what they need AND accomplish more 'value for their money', at that point, they will come to you once more. They are likewise more appreciative than corporate clients.

Up-pitch to Rewriting

For private ventures and experts, each dollar checks, and you may need to persuade them that it IS justified, despite all the trouble to revamp the entire site as opposed to tinker with 'straightforward alter.' Since many clients are sure their words are beautiful... they need editing, or refreshing, or whatever. At that point, your outcast viewpoint can turn out to be helpful as you should pressure the need to rework to suit the reason and objectives of the site. If you can write in 'pyramid' style (most important points first), utilize rational expressions, and direct voice, you will be roads in front of most "I did it without anyone else's help" independent venture sites.

Procure More as an SEO Copywriter

When you can likewise coordinate learning of web crawler permeability; research and utilize one catchphrase state for each page; and recommend page titles, meta depiction, alt labels, and headings, your web copywriting business will move toward becoming SEO copywriting. Search engine optimization copywriting is highly sought after. Thus you can charge more for this work. It, as a rule, includes, at any rate, thirty minutes more research than the official page.

Income at Home - 7 Proven Insider Secrets That Anyone Can Use

1. For long haul achievement never put all your investments tied up in one place. It is excellent and appropriate to cherish your item or opportunity, yet if you need to desert it when that it neglects to be gainful, be happy to give up without thinking back. Once in a while, what looks great on paper isn't that great as a general rule. Enhance, have 2, 3, or even four items or openings. If one comes up short, you have the other three to fall back on.

2. The quickest and most straightforward approach to be fruitful is through Joint Ventures. A Joint Venture is a trade of one accomplice's assets with another. Joint Ventures are an approach to use each accomplice's money, customers, select in records, marketing, and believability to the advantage of both.

3. Right Internet marketing is to convey the correct item using the proper direct mail advertisement to the specific market, and you have it taken care of. The key to capitalizing on your endeavor is to initially change over your offering (item, administration, movement) into a genuine Internet offer. Ensure you have some digital advertising. Sell an answer. Gather all materials into a "how to" EBook. Sought after items are identified with what individuals need to accomplish in their lives; to get

more cash-flow, to get in shape, personal development, etc. If you can prepare a made sought after item complete with affiliates rights, you will need to complete 15 % of the work and have the option to keep 100% of the benefits. There has never been a quicker method to start turning over advantage over the Internet than by selling data items. Try not to give this open door a chance to cruise you by.

4. Great Sales letters are the key to selling anything on the web. The accomplishment of your direct mail advertisement relies upon whether you ace the expertise of copywriting. Every fruitful deal letter have a couple of common elements that anyone can learn in a genuinely brief timeframe. Take care of an issue. Begin with an eye-catching feature. Pose an inquiry in the function. "Do You Need More Money"? Let them know in the subheader the appropriate response is in a letter. "We Will Tell You How To Make More Money, Read On" Get to the point directly at the start of the, so you don't lose them. "Download the Free EBook." Their concern is your chance.

5. There are several key ingredients to making a site that boosts your primary concern. Your website should have an incredible feature. Make moment enthusiasm with an astonishing opening sentence. It ought to have projectiles

posting the advantages. It ought to have healthy streaming passages. Claim to the feelings and recount stories. Concentrate consideration on the highlighted results of your site. Keep your message trustworthy with acceptable tributes. It ought to be flawless and proficient and coherent with brisk stacking. Include high esteem, ease rewards. What's more, finally, it ought to have an email capture system utilizing an autoresponder.

6. Get some free promoting through composing Ezine articles, solo emails, YouTube recordings, interfaces, Craig's rundown, and index submitters. You will discover them on the Internet — all at no expense.

7. To wrap things up, encircle yourself with a portion of the top advertisers on the Internet. You will discover them on Internet marketing gatherings. Talk with them, pose inquiries, and model yourself after them.

Copywriting For The Rest Of Us: 7 Rules You Cannot Ignore

Copywriting appears to be cryptic dark artistry. However, it's shockingly simple to get to grasps with a couple of nuts and bolts. A little at any given moment in a consistent manner will bring exceptional outcomes when you center around the procedures that others have utilized before you. Here are some straightforward principles to enable you to art compelling copy:

Guideline #1

Continuously test. It's called split testing. Regardless of whether your full first direct mail advertisement or deals page changes over 90% of your perusers, continue attempting new thoughts. More straightforward content, illustrations, content shading - anything you can change, change it.

Standard #2

Comprehend who your peruser is. What age and sex would they say they are? Where do they live and what do they work? Is it accurate to say that they are glad? What do they need throughout everyday life? Copywriting is tied in with mixing feelings. A good copywriter will see how the theme to be more than likely a profitable one. Go to a few article directories and read a couple of articles in your picked specialty.

Presently make a lead magnet otherwise called a moral influence that you can giveaway at no expense to allure individuals to join your list. This lead magnet should instruct somebody yet not how to do it. Your paid item will do that!

Set up a squeeze page with a compelling headline, a sentence or two as a presentation, a few bulleted advantages found inside your lead magnet and a solid invitation to take action.

Direct people to your squeeze page utilizing either free or paid techniques.

Consistently part message everything including your headline, bulleted focuses, hues, the content on your suggestion to take action catches, illustrations, and so forth to find what performs best.

Next, go to Google AdWords Keyword Tool to locate a profitable subspecialty. Enter a spending limit of $10 every day. Pick the United States and Canada as your area.

Next, enter your picked specialty as a watchword. Snap on the 'More Like This' catch' Then take a gander at what different catchphrases are shown. These will be your subspecialties. Snap on the 'More Like This' Button for considerably more watchwords.

Hope to perceive how well known every watchword is. Pick one that has at any rate 10,000 indexed lists as these will be specialties individuals are keen on.

When you recognize what subspecialty you need to manufacture your business around, you should accomplish more research to discover what issues individuals are as of now encountering and what individuals are discussing.

Do this by joining gatherings in your specialty and perusing what individuals are discussing. Take a gander at the titles of books on destinations, for example, Amazon and ClickBank. If somebody has composed a paper regarding the matter, they have done research and observed that item will profit his peruser. Sympathy with his prospect implies he will realize how to enable his peruser to perceive how the thing will benefit them.

Principle #3

Use digits. There is something magnetic about "Find 3 Essential Methods of Tax Avoidance," which appears much more compelling than "Find Three Essential Methods... "Maybe this is because we are dependable in a rush that they make sense of stands where the content doesn't. Intuitively, the sign to the peruser is that they can discover the time in their bustling timetable to peruse something short.

Guideline #4

Be enthusiastic. Utilize emotive words and articulations. Indeed, even designers are individuals as well! Claim to the feelings gets your prospect to purchase. Line it up with statistical data points to enable your client to excuse their buy as something they bought for a logical reason.

Standard #5

Make interest. Try not to recount the entire story in the synopsis. Tell your perusers what you are going to train them if they purchase the item, yet don't broadly expound. Reveal to them that on page 15, they will gain proficiency with the insider privileged insights behind monstrous tomato development, however, don't tell them precisely how it's accomplished until they get your item.

Principle #6

Make a shortage. Regardless of whether it's a digital download, figure out how to make your item rare. Without deficit, your peruser will figure they can return and get it some other time. In the realm of information overload, we live in today, that is not going to occur. Making a limited number available at a low cost, or undeniably limited accessibility will goad your perusers to progress toward becoming activity takers. Another strategy to do this is to compensate the item's first buyers with a reward.

Guideline #7

Transform negatives into positives. Recognize any disadvantages your item has before any other individual can. Change the problem into a positive, for example, "this gadget will stop up and keep any additional washing powder in its center, yet that will spare your garments from turning out stained."

Searching For Sales-Letter Copywriters? Peruse This First!

In case you list most business people, you've no uncertainty been sold on this fantasy of the enchanted forces of the sales-letter, and particularly of the sales-letter marketing specialist. He comes in, composes another mystical sales-letter and BAM, your sales experience the rooftop, isn't that so?

It is conceivable. I need you to acknowledge something. This is farfetched. Without a doubt, procuring copywriters and doing sales-letters can be an incredible technique, yet I need to help you to remember reality. This is a long-held insider mystery. Sales-letters are not generally the best decision for an item or business. Ever wonder why no corporations use sales letters? It is anything but a mishap.

It is not as necessary as:

- Little organization = sell-through sales letters

- Huge organization = sell through shop-format

- In fact, in your very own business, there are presumably numerous occasions where you have to explore different avenues regarding and think about what items you could sell through various settings. Copywriters will never let you know of this, yet numerous things are appropriate for a different format of selling.

- So how would you discover your sales-letter marketing specialist, without getting ripped off?

- Have you chosen you do require a sales-letter for this one item? What's more, you need to locate the most ideally equipped man for the activity? Here's the least difficult, come up short evidence approach to discover him.

- Approach your business associates for proposals

- Meeting every one of the prospects you have

- Notice if they demand to complete a sales letter or you were contracting them

For what reason is this significant, and how can it matter if you avert this?

It's obvious, unexpectedly, the best sales-letter copywriters on the planet don't demand that you procure them. They're picky in what and for whom they'll work. Their primary motivation is astonishing outcomes. They're dependent on their specialty, and authority of the abilities.

When they complete a counsel with you (and they all demand a meeting before hiring)... They will test you to discover what they can accomplish for your business. If they find that they can contribute substantially to your primary concern, will they propose keeping in touch with you a decent sales-letter?

So get a counsel with a quality publicist, and see whether you need another sales-letter in any case. If you do, enlist the person who was most fearful about the thought in any case. Unexpected. However, it works.

Copywriting Secrets That the Pros Don't Want You to Know

Did you realize that certain copywriting secrets can detonate your outcomes? There are little things that you can change about your sales duplicate that can effectively affect your transformations and sales. When you are experiencing difficulty creating sales pages that are successful, at that point, you have to continue perusing, and you will get familiar with the copywriting secrets that the experts and the 'masters' don't need you to know.

If you are copywriting on the web, at that point, you should utilize a feature. This is your opportunity to catch the eye of your perusers. If they aren't pulled in to your page immediately, at that point, it doesn't make a difference how incredible the remainder of your duplicate is because they will leave rapidly. There is simply a lot out there on the web for somebody to remain and peruse a page that does not immediately intrigue them.

Along these lines, consider what advantage your item gives that would sound fascinating a planned client. It is safe to say that you are focusing on sales towards people that need to acquire money? Is it true that you are focusing on sales towards people that have skin inflammation? Reveal to them something like, "Progressive Acne Treatment Removes Blemishes In Just One Day!" You need to get to the meat in all respects rapidly. To help catch the eye, talk straightforwardly to the peruser - endeavor to include the word 'you' into your title if you can.

The piece of a sales page after the feature is known as the sales letter. Now and then your whole duplicate is a sales letter, as in email showcasing, so it is an essential piece of the copy. Here is a standout amongst the important copywriting secrets that you will ever hear - every good deal letters are stories! People romantic tales. They want to tune in to stories, and they want to respond to stories.

So make your sales letter a story with a starting, center, and end. Tell the story of somebody (best you) who had an issue. Perhaps they had awful skin inflammation, or they experienced difficulty paying the lease since they had no money. Ensure that you talk about how terrible things were. You got into battles in secondary school since children ridiculed you and your 'hole face.' Or then again you feared opening bills since you realized that your ledger was vacant. Indeed lay it on thick. It helps if these accounts are valid. Copywriting isn't always about recounting to original stories - yet you should speak the truth about your item's advantages! When you lie about what your item can do, you'll pay for it later.

After you talk about how terrible things were for you, you have to discuss the day that you happened upon the answer to your issues. Perhaps somebody said something that gave you thought for a skin inflammation treatment. Or on the other hand, possibly you got so tired of your money related circumstance that you conceptualized for a considerable length of time until you at extended last made sense of an answer.

At that point, talk about how that arrangement tackled the majority of your issues. Your face cleared up in a week, and you were cast a ballot 'most attractive' in your group. Or then again perhaps you set aside up enough cash to travel to Hawaii. You don't need to lay this on excessively thick. However, you need to get the point over that it was your answer that tackled your issues. At that point, reveal to them that you made an item to impart your response to other people - this is your item!

Here is another jewel of a copywriting secret - people love mysteries. If you talk up your answer, however, don't let them know precisely what it is, at that point, it's a secret. Reveal to them that you will impart your secret to them within your item. Your item is the way to your secret arrangement. When your machine is a secret, people feel like it must be important. Try not to be excessively obscure with your strategies or else people will surrender. So share a bit, however, don't discharge the majority of the data.

The Secret and Success of Copywriting in a Network Marketing Business

What is the mystery such vast numbers of system markets have attempted and demonstrated to be effective unfailingly? The secret is copywriting.

What is copywriting, you may inquire? Copywriting is the demonstration of utilizing words to request a particular reaction from your prospects.

Which necessarily implies it is persuasiveness in print. This is mind-boggling because it gives you a MASSIVE influence on your business.

Consider it like this. What number of individuals would you be able to contribute an hour through phone if your pitch states, 15 minutes in length? Four, and no more. Presently, the country you changed over your pitch into a composed message, saying a similar thing as the oral pitch, however in print. Directly what number of individuals would you be able to contribute an hour using email? The highest number of as you can send that email to that is staggering!

Ever been stood up before for an arrangement to demonstrate "the arrangement?"

Nearly everybody has until they become familiar with the mysteries of structure their business with the influence of copywriting and web showcasing.

There are just 24 hours in a day, so you MUST have influence working for you in your business if you ever need to accomplish riches in this industry.

Influence is the reason you got in system advertising in any case, yet amusingly you were not instructed how to use your prospecting endeavors, copywriting and email promoting are the influence you need.

Since we realize what the mystery is, we have to understand how to use it appropriately. Poor copywriting will get you nowhere, however fruitful copywriting will extend and develop your business quicker than you suspected conceivable.

One of the critical components most system advertisers miss, even the individuals who think about copywriting, is that you should:

Realize Your Target Market Intimately and Give Them What They Want.

In the event that your objective market is individuals experiencing diabetes, and you have an item that can enable you to need to comprehend what diabetes is, the means by which it impacts individuals, how your item impacts individuals who have diabetes (not what your item does, however how the individual that uses your item feels).

By understanding your objective market, you can all the more likely compose and set up your duplicate (your composed pitch). Get inside your actual market's head. If you need to pitch something to somebody, you need to profess to be them, make sense of their sentiments, what is imperative to them. This will be vital to the accomplishment of your duplicate.

How might you start using this in your system advertising business today? There are numerous ways. However, a straightforward one composes an email about your item or open door utilizing the abilities talked about above. Keep in mind, don't just pitch somebody your article or opportunity, give them accommodating, intelligent data.

How to put it all together to build trust in prospects and close the sale

Sadly, a few prospects see a sales call as an intrusion upon their day, and interference from the significant things they need to do. Except if they consider you to be indispensable to giving the appropriate responses hello look for, the items they need or the arrangements they need. You should abstain from appearing to be an interloper, a sick person, or a period squanderer.

Building trust with the purchaser depends on the best possible methodology and not commanding the discussion.

In expert selling, building trust is more significant than being preferred. A lethal blemish for salespeople happens when they trust that they have to 'pitch themselves' to the imminent customer. This isn't right; it is 'outdated' and drives salespeople to inevitably overselling themselves and losing the trust of the prospect.

You have to know and comprehend that being trusted is genuinely more profitable than being loved when selling. When you're believed, it, by and large, pursues that you'll be preferred. You have to abstain from looking for an endorsement. This doesn't in any case; imply that you ought to be discourteous, hostile, or grating. It likewise doesn't mean that you should be excessively forceful, overwhelm the discussion or be overly well disposed of, too early, either.

Neglect to position yourself firmly and a few prospects will consent to see you be a considerate or just act of goodwill some help. Except if you can change both of these attitudes quickly, you'll never go anyplace with your prospects.

That implies you should initially lessen pressure quickly. What's more, no doubt about it; there will dependably be pressure in any sales circumstance.

Prospects can peruse you like a book. They can right away detect your confidence, your frame of mind about selling, your faith in your items and administrations, and your solace level with them. It appears in your eyes, motions, developments, and manner of speaking. When you don't unwind, they won't unravel. If you can't decrease the pressure among you, you'll never get to the trust level that is required. Trust is everything.

Why Building Trust is Necessary For a Successful Network Marketing Business

The best system showcasing entrepreneurs will reveal to you that the way to their prosperity was their capacity to make a relationship of trust with the general population they supported into their association. You have to sell your prospect on yourself first, and after that manufactured an association with that client until they have the motivation to stay faithful to you. To offer yourself and assemble a fruitful system promoting business, you have to concentrate totally on the prospect. Try not to focus on yourself, your business, and your items. Instead, you have to find out about your prospects needs and needs by posing the correct inquiries.

Active system advertisers likewise keep up their honesty consistently and convey what they guarantee. Ensure that you are dependable, never oversell and under-convey, and furthermore ensure that you don't make any reasons when something incorrectly or startling occurs. This is vital to building that fruitful system advertising business.

When building trust, you have to establish a generally excellent connection from the earliest starting point and focus on both your verbal and nonverbal abilities and body language. Individuals will give close consideration to your body language and how you present yourself. Here are a few different ways you can improve your nonverbal abilities:

1) Project a positive picture - You don't' have to spend a fortune on garments, however, ensure you are top notch and dressed appropriately for the group of onlookers you might want to draw in.

2) Stand certainly - Make beyond any doubt you have an erect posture, and abstain from slumping over. Standing straight with reasonable posture projects confidence.

3) Make eye to eye connection with your prospect - When you are conversing with somebody, ensure you give them eye to eye connection. When you look at your chance in

the eye, they will get the inclination that they can confide in you.

4) Smile - If you are excited about something, look like it, grin and be energized.

When you make little modifications and improvements in these territories of nonverbal correspondence, you will have a more grounded possibility of structure connections and picking up trust from your prospects. When you gain their confidence, they will turn out to be more pulled in to you, and in the long run, become a devoted client or sign up as a wholesaler for your business. This is exceptionally basic when building an effective system promoting business.

Tips on How to Build Trust and Your Business

Is your present showcasing methodology helping you acquire as much as you'd like?

Does your promoting plan help you create new prospects every week and after that convert them to paying customers?

It is safe to say that you are getting the main concern results you need from your promoting endeavors?

To get the outcomes you need, your customers must trust you, have confidence in you first, and after that in your items or administrations. Studies have demonstrated that individuals purchase from those that they know, as and trust. Your customers need to buy from organizations that surpass their image guarantee. Who goes past the normal? Who shock their clients by showing a dimension of duty one, by and large, connect with family.

You wouldn't purchase a vehicle when you didn't figure it could get you home. Nor would buy a car from a vendor you thought was ransacking you on the cost or if the seller probably won't remain behind the motor if it dropped out as you drove it off the part. The following are 6.5 tips on the best way to build trust and build your business.

1. Over-convey to Get Referrals

When you need a specialist or legal counselor or an incredible eatery, you approach a companion for a referral. You solicit because you trust the recommendations from individuals you know. Try not to believe that the infrequent reference will come in suddenly. When you emerge from the rest by going well beyond what a client expects, it makes it simpler to actualize a customer referral framework to create new referrals.

2. Get Testimonials

Having qualifications are incredible, having much experience is far and away superior, yet individuals give more consideration to what others need to state about you. Get the telephone and call your clients to solicit what they thought from your items or administrations, what they loved about it and how it was useful. You can alter their remarks and get authorization to utilize the altered comments as tributes in your advertising materials.

3. Give Something Away

When you give individuals something, paying little respect to the cost, they are bound to trust you and give back where its due by purchasing something from you. It is known as the Law of Reciprocity. Make it work for you. You can utilize an E-book, articles, a workshop, teleseminar, or free exhibit to build nature and at last trust in you and your item.

4. Give Examples

Recount to a story as opposed to making claims about your item or administrations. Use contextual analyses to determine what you accomplished for whom and the distinction is made in their life or their business. Use numbers, individuals like data, for example, 'expanded their primary concern by 30 percent. With the real brand story, a brand worth having faith, it won't be overlooked.

5. Customize Your Marketing

Individuals work with individuals. Help prospects become acquainted with you and trust you. Let your passion, professionalism, and character go over in your advertising materials. Incorporate an image of yourself, with a grin, in a prominent place on your promoting materials... in any case, not on your business card. When you're at a convention or other applicable occasions, share this data on your blog, tweets, and other online life outlets.

6. Keep in contact

The general population you see and converse with all the time are usually the ones you trust the most. Correspondence is a crucial element for creating trust. If you sell administrations or top of the line items, a personal telephone call is a standout amongst the ideal approaches to address prospects' inquiries and to build trust. Keep up contact with your prospects and customers usually and request their assessment.

6.5. Lessen Perceived Risk and Provide Value and Benefits

A buyers' most significant concern is how well your item or administration will perform. Giving a certification has a significant effect, yet as a rule, it won't make the deal. You should explain the esteem and after that characterize the advantages you give. Make sure to express your duty to see that your customers are cheerful, yet blissful about your item and administrations.

Ways on Building Trust With Your List for Sales Generation

One of the benefits a company can have is a rundown or arrangements of imminent customers and clients. In any case, the inquiry is how you might guarantee that the prospects in your outline will purchase your products and not that of your rival? Individuals buy or look for the administrations from those organizations that they know, trust, and like, so it is best that you construct an association with your rundown by setting up a trust.

Have a Consistent Behavior

Having a steady behavior is the initial phase in structure trust with clients and customers. You need to detect those individuals with erratic behavior as they are those that you ought not to manufacture trust, particularly with regards to setting up a business relationship. This sort of individuals will, in general, accomplish something bizarre or insane, so you need to maintain a strategic distance from these individuals with regards to business.

All individuals have companions who they discover incredibly intriguing. Although they will, in general, go insane, however, the fun and good company as it is their behavior. Furthermore, when they began to act straight directly like a bolt more often than not, you would believe that something incorrectly is transpiring. So on the off chance that you are attempting to fabricate an association with your rundown of prospects, clients or endorsers, having a positive behavior is an absolute necessity with the goal for you to realize how to deal with them when they speak with you.

Be More Believable

Being reasonable is the second thing that you ought to have to construct an association with your rundown. You should realize that occasionally the fact of the matter isn't credible is someone hears it out of the blue as they don't have any foundation learning on what you are discussing. In this occurrence, backing off is the best alternative for you to do, and you need to reveal to them enough that they will accept what you have said. It is exceptionally fundamental in authenticity. If you need others to trust you, don't overhype things.

Presenting Good Quality Products

If you need individuals to confide in your business, furnish them with products just as administrations, which are high in quality. It is a definite purpose behind you to manufacture trust with your rundown. In joint ventures, you likewise need to ensure that the products or administrations that you will acquaint with them are of good quality as it will speak to you and your company. If they are not good, it will think about your company.

Review Products Honestly

Another approach to construct an association with your rundown is giving your assessment just as the underwriting of products. If you direct item reviews, you ought to do it sincerely, and you should go through them to accompany the best possible and fair review of the item you embrace.

Offering Association to Influential Individuals

Building more trust is likewise achievable by referencing companions or associates of an impact yet not in a promotion way, except if you by and by knowing the individual. Be genuine and shared when your home base or eat with them. You must be careful of who you eat with as individuals will do prejudge you dependent on the general population you are with.

Simple techniques to turn your bad business marketing into an irresistible copy

If you feel that viral promoting is something that sounds strangely awful, quit trusting that, because popular showcasing is something worth being thankful for. So great truth be told, that these seven viral advertising methods to help your online business that I am going to uncover soon, will undoubtedly change your company because of the intensity of traffic age they will bring to your destinations. They will likewise disentangle your showcasing by the viral impact of straightforward and moment transmission of messages from individual to individual.

This simple and moment transmission of messages from individual to individual does ultimately work, mainly when the proposal to advance the word originates from a giving beginning stage first. That is you offer a rebate or a value cut, a vital report free direct in return for sharing that data to a partner or companion. Keep your proposals, offers, limits, free reports, and so forth very significant to what you need to request that your prospects do which for this situation is to share your substance virally.

Asking your loved ones to advance something without giving them motivation for doing as such isn't getting down to business well. So the appropriate response is to offer high essential data that merits sharing.

Also, what is this useful data we are discussing here? Peruse further for approaches to spread information effectively.

1. Beginning with blogging, for example, you can have different marketers interfacing with you and participating

in the viral promoting expected to advance your message for new and existing items and administrations. Your website can provide the devices and the showcasing for spreading your word across the web.

2. With the formation of digital books, that is, advertising with the content or a promoting digital magazine, that has pictures just as content, and connections to different locales or your very own site, you can get a lot of viral traffic to whatever online virtual property you need. Instruct your perusers how and with your material for sharing it effectively. You can present your digital books on digital book catalogs regularly for nothing; this gives you a lot of showcasing viral power, because of your prospects' eagerness to convey your free substance to their following supporters.

3. Another excellent method for conveying free data to pick up a bit of leeway with viral advertising is to utilize cell phones. Even though the populace everywhere is currently adroit at separating publicizing, there is as yet a great opportunity with this medium. There are simple promoting procedures that you can apply to influence the prospect to pass on data to their devotees or companions. Utilizing instant messages, for example, is a powerful method for

imparting a free offer, or administration, reaction, challenges, and so on.

4. The Internet makes it conceivable to utilize record sharing, and this is exceptionally valuable for viral advertising as well. Such a significant number of individuals are going on the web for downloading video files, content files, sound record, and free programming files. This implies there is an excellent opportunity for marketers to utilize this medium virally. Offer free downloads in different configurations that your clients will pass on, sharing them to their companions, family, and supporters of lift your promoting message to a large number even a large number of individuals. Picture you composing and playing out a tune that you record as an MP3 that you send to a companion. His companion tunes in to it prefer it, and he sends it to his companions... It would not take well before your theme is in numerous individuals' hard drives. This is the intensity of viral showcasing.

5. What about eMail showcasing at that point? Similarly, as I said before in section 3 primarily messaging in your specialty requesting that they pass on your message, isn't getting down to business appropriately because that isn't the right method for doing viral advertising. Instead,

incorporate a joke, or an MP3 record, a free report very focused on their interests or a video, and you will see the kick that viral advertising provides for your crusade. All that is worth-while accomplishing for your prospects since those things are excellent material to pass on.

6. What else would you be able to utilize that creates buzz and makes individuals forward your substance? Maybe using forums will do it, indeed, when you use unobtrusive advertising procedures, nonintrusive, separated, without any preparation and cautious strategies in discussions, will function admirably for you. The key here is to not hurry into showcasing. Individuals in forums won't see eye to eye to promoting in their space, so your methodology should be estimated, aware and un-rushed so that after the basis is set, advantages and results will begin to occur for you. For savvy marketers, forums provide another excellent opportunity for viable viral showcasing.

7. Different strategies can go here for snowballing the showcasing message — for example, re-marking digital books, for instance. First obviously, ensure you have the right for doing as such, and afterward, you can give them away unreservedly. Or then again you can compose articles with connections to free material that you can pass on to your prospects and them to their endorsers...

There is a great deal you can do via hunting on the web down marking privileges of items that you would then be able to advance to your clients for nothing, and they like this, pass them on to their companions and prospects, making again another viral advertising effort.

Also, kindly, don't imagine that these are everything you can do; there are different methods, in certainty, numerous strategies that you can use in your promoting to cause them to circulate the web. The web search tools can give you a considerable amount of data about them. At any rate, endeavor to execute these seven viral showcasing methods to help your online business.

Showcasing With Articles Will Give Your Online Business The Exposure It Needs

The internet or the internet is the best spot to do showcasing. The purpose of this is evident because billions of individuals surf the internet every day. In light of this reality, you would now be able to change your nearby business into a global phenomenon and skyrocket your income rapidly. Along these lines, increasingly more entrepreneurs are currently taking a gander at the internet for business developments.

Promoting through the assistance of the internet sounds truly encouraging; however, the primary issue that most entrepreneurs face is that they don't have the foggiest idea where to begin the procedure. Along these lines, a large portion of them feels that they're going to require a massive spending plan if they need to get their business name uncovered online. This is false. There are loads of approaches to showcase a business online, and some of them are even free, and you can utilize them boundlessly. Article promotion is one of the free advertising techniques that you can use online. Also though article promotion is open, the outcomes that it can create regarding the business presentation are genuinely encouraging. The more significant part of internet marketers nowadays will reveal to you that articles are the ideal approach in case you're extremely genuine about getting known over the globe using the internet. As its name infers, article promotion is the way toward composing articles about the items or administrations that a specific business foundation brings to the table. Furthermore, the procedure likewise includes the accommodation of what is written into article banks or article indexes.

By composing substance and posting them in various indexes online, organizations will almost certainly lead end clients to their sites through the assistance of back connections. Like this will enable them to expand the number of guests that are dropping by their locales once a day. As a final product, they get the chance to develop their deals and thus their benefits. Substance posts are a success win circumstance since they help both entrepreneurs and individuals who are searching for valuable data. Many individuals nowadays go to the internet to search for data about items and administrations that they are intrigued to buy. Shoppers state this is the "savvy thing" to do. Along these lines, posts done online are boiling material for a lot of web surfers given the necessary data that they provide. This makes positions fill in as scaffolds that associate organizations with forthcoming clients.

When you compose posts, ensure that you incorporate an asset enclose every single one of them. An asset box includes a short description about you and your business just as a backlink that prompts your site. Through the guise of asset boxes, you make yourself the right image online.

Posts are amazing themselves, yet it's never awful to include something that will give a lift such that these

Copywriting is the thing that brings the client and the organization together to discover what the two of them need. Website optimization copywriters produce content, similar to an article, that talks about your business or administrations in an engaging and instructive manner that demonstrates to perusers that you are an applicable business. Copywriting additionally utilizes a system called keyword to inquire about that finds what keywords your clients are hunting down, and after that objectives the copywriting towards those clients by joining the keywords.

These keywords are likewise a noteworthy apparatus in improving your remaining with web index results. Since your SEO copywriting administrations will fuse the exact keywords that individuals are scanning for, web crawlers will discover those keywords in your copywriting and take it back to the client. That is a fundamental model of what occurs; nonetheless, it is muddled by different things like keyword thickness, rivalry for that keyword with various organizations, and your site's believability with the web crawler. Utilizing quality copywriting apparatuses after some time will assist you with improvements in these zones.

When you have gotten down to business finding your optimal clients and making your organization known, at that point comes the activity of changing over those beautiful new leads into brings - deals to a close. Website design enhancement copywriting is multifunctional in such a manner since it not just carries your item to the client; it influences the client to push ahead and work with you. Your copywriting substance must be unique, useful, and valuable to the client. At the point when these characteristics are all together, copywriting can be adequately enticing.

Interfacing With Readers Using Emotional Copywriting

With regards to copywriting, understanding essential human instinct goes far toward making deals. The headline on a business duplicate ought to be the underlying consideration grabber. Headlines that are ineffectively made or powerless will execute the impact of global peace. The three reserves of a gripping headline are by and large obvious to peruse, focusing on a specific gathering of people and being productive with the correct keywords.

The direct mail advertisement's body matters as well. It is the meat of any copywriting piece. The organization ought to be implanted with ground-breaking, dynamic words that are short and to the point. The arranging is likewise significant. Highlighting, tables, and shots should all be used to build the visual intrigue and meaningfulness of the piece. Keep in mind, little bits of data are in every case superior to anything long passages; long sections overpower and bore the peruser.

A suggestion to take action is fundamental to any business copywriting letter. An invitation to take action is a technique used to request that the peruser buy an item or administration. The offer ought to be challenging to leave behind and the suggestion to take action ought to incorporate a type of due date. Insights demonstrate that 40 percent of potential clients will delay making a buy.

Specialists suggest that marketing specialists unmistakably express an unconditional promise and a protected installment preparing framework to subdue the peruser's dread of being ripped off or turning into a casualty of wholesale fraud. Approximately 70 percent of leads will verge on making a buy yet flounder ultimately. An excellent copywriting piece will secure the peruser like purchasing the item or administration.

A postscript, or P.S., should whole up the primary concern of the business duplicate and what the per-user needs to recollect about the suggestion to take action. Many individuals check a business duplicate to get the key pieces of data; in this way, a P.S. is completely important. This is likewise the spot to remind perusers what makes the item or administration unique and superior to anything that is offered by contenders.

The correct shading plan additionally assumes an essential job in getting the consideration of perusers. Shading congruity and differentiation hit the peruser on an intuitive dimension. The satisfactory blank area is significant because it offers the watcher's eyes a reprieve. What's more, ladies have an inclination of gaudy hues instead of ho-murmur ones. Yellow is perfect for highlighting key words or expressions, and red is an eye-catching accent shading.

Copywriting Tips for the New Internet Marketer

Everybody has their very own most loved copywriting tips, yet, as another web advertiser, there is exceptionally just a bunch that you should know to get began. What are they, and by what method will they kick you off? How about we see.

In this part, we will view three of the critical things you should think about copywriting in case you're another web advertiser. We'll begin off by becoming more acquainted with your product, pursue that up by becoming more acquainted with your client and finish up by getting your direct mail advertisement out into the enormous full world.

First of the copywriting tips is becoming more acquainted with your product.

What do you think about the product you're selling? In case you're the maker of the product, you should know a reasonable piece, however, in case you're another web advertiser how would you get to a phase where you can unquestionably expound on it? There's just a single way, honestly. Purchase any affiliate product you might advance.

When you conclude that you will advance an expensive extravagance product at that point getting one may not be conceivable, yet most new web advertisers choose to begin somewhat littler than that, in any case.

When you're copywriting, you have to hear what you're saying to pitch to the individual visiting your site. If you don't think about the product, it will appear in duplicate, and for the most part, the general population hoping to purchase will be reasonably educated up about the products they're hoping to purchase. So get it, use it, become a 'specialist' with it.

If you think about the product, you'll have the option to expound on the things that will matter to the purchaser. This will make your life as a publicist a ton simpler.

The second of the copywriting tips is to realize who you're pitching to.

All in all, who are you pitching to? The vast majority now will answer that they're attempting to throw to the same number of individuals as a need to purchase, which, to a limited degree, is most likely right. However, your direct mail advertisement shouldn't talk a gathering of individuals.

To begin with, you ought to compose for only one individual - the individual sitting before their PC screen understanding it. Disregard that you may have many 'one' individuals understanding it at any time treat the peruser as if you are having a coordinated discussion with just them. The individual touch is dependably a victor.

Next, who is this individual you're in discussion with? Most products will focus on a particular statistic; do you know who's in your focused on a statistic? In case you're selling a product called 'Sewing for the Total Bewildered' and fill it brimming with road slang, you're most likely going to miss your objective market of 65multi-year old retirement town grannies by only a touch. Not saying that teen skateboard junkies aren't knitters, yet they'll be in the minority.

If you know your 'individual,' you can pitch the direct mail advertisement at their dimension and address their needs. Direct mail advertisements ought to be loaded up with the advantages of the product (which you'll currently know having utilized it), and the benefits you'll have the option to feature will change to suit you are focused on the group of onlookers.

The remainder of the copywriting tips is to complete something.

It might sound senseless, yet such vast numbers of individuals tumble down at this stage. There are a ton of copywriters, specifically with regards to their very own products, who need to hit the nail on the head the first occasion when that they don't get anything out there in any case.

Nothing is regularly going to be immaculate. Take what you have, get it out to the more extensive world, and cause modifications as you to come. You ought to dependably be trying your duplicate - for instance, split test two adaptations of a feature, at that point utilize the best and split test it with another, this should be possible with all aspects of your direct mail advertisement - you will begin to see territories where you can improve the change rate of the direct mail advertisement.

If you over dissect, to begin with, and don't get anything distributed on your site, you aren't going to go anyplace. Alright, you might not have the best direct mail advertisement, you might not have the best change rate, however despite everything you'll be showing things can provide to you and your business. The extra that I'm conversing with about here is SEO or website improvement. Web optimization includes the utilization of a few techniques that help get a site positioned quickly in web search tools.

Your Simple 3 Step Guide to Success With Your Herbalife Business

Joining a system advertising company has turned out to be increasingly, and that goes for the company Herbalife too. In reality, numerous people join this company, hoping that they can accomplish financial freedom by becoming their very own Herbalife business. Alongside the prospect of becoming economically independent, comes the likelihood to get the existence you have needed continuously lastly transform your fantasies into the real world. People need to accomplish absolute freedom, they need to leave their 8-5 working days behind, and they need to have the option to do anything they desire when they need and with the people they need to be with. These things were the reasons why I joined a system showcasing company a few years prior. I needed to succeed SO seriously, and hence, and I realized that I would accomplish that ultimate freedom and become financially independent - at the same time, something turned out badly.

1. To start with, you have to position yourself as the master! You have to know the company Herbalife and the items and remuneration plan great. However, that isn't sufficient. To turn into the master, you need to realize your group of onlookers too. Who's your objective market?

2. Second, you need trust in Herbalife's items, provided that you don't, your prospects won't feel progressively significant purchasing the items from you. Accordingly, when you need to prevail with your Herbalife business, and it is vital that you like the things yourself.

3. Third, you should be submitted. Succeeding isn't simple, and the active people in this world and furthermore in this industry are a minority. Why? Since a great many people, regardless of their need and want to succeed, end up stopping, since they aren't submitted, and after committing numerous errors, they lose confidence. In this way, if you need to prevail with your Herbalife business, you need to begin considering missteps to be a piece of

succeeding, because you will take in and develop from committing errors.

If you need to succeed, you can - begin instructing yourself in showcasing and quit sitting idle on things that aren't working. When you've figured out how to showcase viably, and you won't let anything stop you, you will prevail with your Herbalife business.

Chapter five

How to make price irrelevant and be the only choice for your ideal customer

If you are thinking about utilizing on the web search tool promoting instruments, you are most likely considering how SEO copywriting administrations truly work. Website optimization copywriting is a significant part of internet searcher showcasing, and probably a standout amongst the most broadly utilized. One reason for what reason is that copywriting works in various regions. Copywriting is persuasive at focusing on your gathering of people of potential clients, upgrading your essence with web crawler results, and changing over leads into deals. The accompanying article will go over a portion of the fundamental techniques for SEO copywriting administrations and how they work to profit your business.

One of the boundaries you most likely face in making your business increasingly productive is in achieving your planned clients. How would you discover the general population that you need to work with? Furthermore, more significantly, how would you get these individuals to find and afterward pick you? This is the place SEO copywriting comes in and gets down to business.

The most significant thing to recall is that copywriting is intended to mirror the whole idea of your business, while in the meantime focusing on the necessities of the clients.

improvement over the general population who don't arrive direct mail advertisements out there to be seen. Begin something that you would then be able to improve.

There you make them copywriting: tips for the new web advertiser. For the more significant part of the general population who are selling on the web, they won't be three of the most progressive things they'll find out about today. However, they will work for them.

Copywriting Business - Make More Money As a Copywriter

How's your copywriting business faring? In case you're not authoring cash in this economic stoppage, you ought to be embarrassed about yourself. This is a great time to be a marketing specialist; admittedly, most publicists are reserved a very long time ahead with customers who are anxious to benefit themselves of copywriting administrations.

Here are three hints which will support you.

1. What Are You Selling? Make a List

Your initial phase in making more cash is to see what administrations you're at present selling. Maybe you're merely selling copywriting deals pages. You can undoubtedly offer a lot more administrations.

At first, you may begin with administrations which are corresponding to an administration you're as of now selling. For instance, in case you're selling a private venture copywriting administrations, consider what the business is endeavoring to accomplish, and how you can assist the company with achieving it.

Many private ventures are losing cash, and don't know it.

2. Tell Clients The best way to Stop Bleeding Money

You can broaden your copywriting administrations when you tell your clients the best way to maintain their businesses all the more adequately.

Here's a little model. A considerable lot of your clients as of now have email records. Anyway, the odds are that they once in a while contact the general population on this rundown. I've never met a customer who IS utilizing his mailing list.

When you can demonstrate your customer that conveying ordinary email messages will expand his business benefits, you just did another copywriting work for yourself in sending those standard email messages.

3. "Retainer": the Magic Word

What number of your customers have you on a retainer? In a perfect world, in any event, 10 of your customers ought to have you on a retainer, so they're sure that you are prepared willing and ready to do copywriting for them whenever of the day or the week - even on ends of the week.

Make a rundown of the advantages to your clients of having you on retainer. You'll be stunned at how appealing this is to numerous customers.

Particularly in these straitened economic times, numerous organizations have cut their promoting offices down deep down. This implies there is a lot of work for independent publicists. You should make your customers mindful of what you can do, and the advantages of having you like a semi individual from staff.

A simple framework to help you blast through writer's block and know exactly what to say in any piece of writing

Truly, copywriting, particularly the first kind, is a created expertise and not a natural one. It isn't fundamental that a person who has a post-advanced education in English or some other language is an excellent copywriter and the opposite side of the coin is that a good or excellent copywriter needn't bother with quite a bit of phonetic training to be fruitful. So, the properties that make a good copywriter are his comprehension of the specialty, knowledge of the focused on perusers and his background's in general. Give us a chance to take a gander at these perspectives in more prominent detail...

Comprehension of the specialty: If one is composing a duplicate about a specific hobby, state the oil business, the copywriter needs to comprehend the specialty either by experience or by temperance of nitty-gritty research. An expert copywriter isn't required to have involvement in each specialty, so the last holds good. Generally, the individual in question needs excellent research aptitudes and a ravenous hunger for information... The more introduction a copywriter gets to the specialty, the better his duplicate will be.

Comprehension of focused perusers: Readers might be conventional as in newspapers or magazines or present day as in a web-based distributing. Whatever the classification of perusers, a good copywriter needs a good comprehension of his peruser base and adjust his phonetic just as articulation aptitudes to oblige their preferences and intelligibility. Utilizing specialty arranged language would help, however holding that to a lower level is prudent. As in the above precedent, an oil specialty expert would get "smooth" uniquely in contrast to an individual outside the specialty. In this way, a good copywriter needs to comprehend his objective perusers and modify his style to make the duplicate look "smooth" and make it stick where it should.

Experience: A look or a viewpoint or a knowledge into individuals is significant for a good copywriter. Even though it might appear to be irrelevant to a new copywriter or one who isn't a copywriter, and a little experience will demonstrate something else... A good copywriter is a person who claims to all perusers somewhat or the other, establishing the required connection among the intended interest group. To confirm that connection, the individual needs to comprehend the psychological cosmetics by placing himself into their shoes. This comes just with involvement, and this experience is the way to turning into a good copywriter.

In this manner, turning into a functional and expert copywriter isn't generally a scholarly procedure, yet a good copywriter turns out to be better by composing ceaselessly and by picking up involvement in various specialties and various types of target gathering of people.

5 Tips to Get More Prospects to Trust What You Say

The third means to the seven insider facts of publicizing is to get more prospects to believe what you state. Assume that nobody trusts you. Presently, that sounds rather obtuse, isn't that right? Individuals don't have any acquaintance with you so for what reason would they accept what you state?

Presently you will likewise have heard that individuals purchase from individuals they know, as and trust so here are five essential hints to fabricate believe that you can put to utilize immediately.

1. Use Photos

You could begin with your photograph in your promotion or on your site and an inscription underneath that. Individuals would then be able to see you and get a feeling of association. That is an extremely, ground-breaking approach to construct trust.

Photographs of your customers are extraordinary as well. It's encouraging to see that others have just put their trust in you. Furthermore, if you have an unmistakable item or can exhibit your administration in real life, incorporate a photograph so individuals can perceive what it resembles. This immediate ads substance to your offer and confirmation that it's genuine.

When you have blocks and mortar business incorporate an image of your structure and staff as proof.

2. Genuine Copy

Utilize the exact duplicate to uncover the official explanation for what you are doing or advertising. Initially, it's emotive, and we realize that individuals purchase on feeling. In any case, similarly as significant is your legitimacy will radiate through in your words and that is genuine, acculturating. Individuals will consequently feel like they can believe you to do what you state.

3. Solid Guarantee

You basically should have a reliable certification. You can not go past, making it an easy decision to work with you.

What are you arranged to do by method for certification, if you don't satisfy your guarantees? Tell individuals they have nothing to lose and everything to pick up by purchasing your administration or item.

Presently days it's insufficient to offer an unconditional promise. That is guaranteed. You have to show that you will be the failure if your item does not satisfy desires, not them.

In all actuality, not many individuals will take you up on your certification; however, it will build your deals since you have shown your dependability.

4. Tributes

Presently, a standout amongst the most dominant things you can do to get individuals to believe you is to assemble your believability through tributes. You can't merely circumvent blowing your own trumpet constantly. What other individuals state about you is pure enchantment.

You get moment believability and verification when another person is approving what you state.

You could utilize those in composed structure with an image or meeting someone. Inquire as to yourself and use the sound or you could video them - significantly progressively incredible.

So don't consider tributes similarly as a thank you letter that you got. You could even make your own. Help someone compose or talk about you such that will bolster what it is you need to impart to other individuals — ground-breaking stuff.

5. Proof your expertise

Numerous entrepreneurs are unassuming and humble and don't generally need to discuss themselves and blow their own horns.

With regards to something like posting your experience and your expertise and explicit capabilities, you basically should tell your peruser. They won't know generally.

Try not to take cover behind it. When you've at any point accomplished it - share it and assemble that dimension of trust that you can, and will do what you state.

Presently put a few of these tips to work for you, and you will build your client's trust and increment your deals. When you have their confidence, you can take a shot at getting more individuals to regard your esteem. Sounds similar - however, it's not something very identical by any stretch of the imagination.

Copywriting Choices - Specialist or Non-Specialist?

Let's be honest: copywriting is a reasonably 'specialty' occupation. Relatively few people outside the advertising field think a lot about it. Alright, they may realize that copywriters write scripts for understood TV plugs or press advertisements. Weight them to take it any further, and there's usually a resonating quietness!

It's protected to state that copywriting is an 'authority' profession. So for what reason would the contention emerge about the benefits or generally of an expert or non-authority copywriter? The general observation is that copywriting is now particular enough many thanks. Possibly it's human instinct - or the idea of our over-created Capitalist economies - to need to make new sub-sets of obscure ranges of abilities.

By the by, divisions and separations do exist. Also, that is in a field without the precise scope of the law or bookkeeping which spread pretty much every dimension of our general public to incorporate authorities, for example, separation or business legal counselors, scientific or charge bookkeepers - to give some cases.

To anybody outside the advertising scene, a copywriter writes words that help associations expose themselves, their items as well as administrations up until this point, so great. As a copywriter, you're relied upon to have the option to write whatever's 'business.' The specialism is set up - and copywriting is a non-authority or 'generalist' ability with numerous applications.

Touch the most superficial layer, in any case, and it before long turns out to be confident that the universe of advertising and promoting is a perplexing mosaic of systems and abilities that work distinctively in various market sectors and with different target groups of onlookers. It is this assorted variety with which copywriting and copywriters are tested.

It's presumably all the more lighting up to take a gander at this from the entirely different points of view of associations who need to augment their interest in copywriting aptitudes, and copywriters who might think about whether further specialization is attractive or suitable as a 'lifelong move.'

Likewise, with most different callings, it's a sensible presumption that most copywriters begin off as 'generalists.' Along these lines, they will become familiar with the ropes and discover which parts of the specialty are most speaking to them by and by - and in which perspectives they exceed expectations. This incorporates aptitudes, for example, direct mail advertisement composing, website copywriting, advertising concepts, media relations, and a hundred different things.

Another thought emerges before taking the specialization course. This identifies with specific market sectors, a significant number of which have their novel requests. Property sector copywriting, for example, is colossally not quite the same as composing for the IT or telecoms sectors, while money related copywriting requires a very surprising establishing from, state, travel copywriting.

A few copywriters practice since they have a long haul enthusiasm for vehicles, travel, or some other pastime. They may have been utilized beforehand in an industry that gave the ideal foundation to turn into an expert copywriter in that field.

One more course to touching base as an expert copywriter must be depicted as 'inadvertent.' Numerous copywriters pick copywriting as a vocation since they have a characteristic familiarity with words, or they know somebody in the business who gave them work.

Throughout the following couple of minutes we will be examining how to fulfill your customers requirements for your copywriting jobs by; adding character to your direct mail advertisement, the significance of what you state over the crease, benefits for your direct mail advertisement, how to not leave your prospects in obscurity, and how to appropriately converse with your guests.

1 - Copywriting jobs tip - Adding character to your direct mail advertisement:

It's imperative to recollect while composing for your copywriting jobs, do not fear to share your excitement, just as enabling your watchers to become more acquainted with you on an increasingly close to home dimension. Including character inside your duplicate will allow your prospects to see that you're a genuine individual that they can associate with. Since you can't be directly before them, you have to display your duplicate such that will welcome your prospects "With a comforting grin."

2 - Copywriting occupation tip - Do not utilize "We":

A ton of entrepreneurs feels that it's progressively expert to state "we" inside their duplicate, regardless of whether they're the main ones that run the site. You should be glad for your work and your item, and state "I" as much as you can all through your direct mail advertisement.

3 - Learning to enthrall your watchers over the overlay:

One of the most significant things that expert marketing specialists use in their copywriting jobs is to catch their watcher's enthusiasm over the overlay. Over the overlay implies the space that your watchers can see before looking down. If this area lacks in drawing in your prospects to peruse further, at that point bid a fond farewell as they are going to hit the back catch.

4 - Copywriting jobs tip - Use the same number of advantages as you can inside your direct mail advertisement:

The general population who land the most copywriting positions see very well indeed that the benefits are what sell the item. You genuinely need to target what your client will search for from your item. Discover the responses to this inquiry by posing to yourself from the "how might this benefit me" perspective.

5 - Important copywriting jobs tip - Leave nothing out:

When composing your duplicate, ensure you have it mapped out not to leave anything to your prospects creative energy. Lay everything out before them so they won't ponder about you not conveyed in a particular area. Help them to remember how the highlights will improve a fantastic nature.

Discover Why You Need to Learn Internet Copywriting

Internet copywriting can be scary, particularly for entrepreneurs who don't believe themselves to be "scholars." Getting the hang of copywriting and applying it to your business site can and will build your benefit in gaining potential.

We have all heard the familiar maxim, "It's not what you state; however, how you state it." An expertly composed message can be instrumental in helping your business succeed. Why? With the end goal for individuals to become more acquainted with your item, comprehend your administration, and come to believe what you are letting them know, you should communicate in a manner that is clear, compact and separates your business.

The way to progress is to apply your insight to the craft of site copywriting. An elegantly composed site will create income by drawing in new clients with an energizing and tempting message, keeping up current clients with a dependable and acceptable tone, and separating your business from the challenge.

That is the reason it is critical to get familiar with the ability to copywrite as an entrepreneur. Try not to be terrified or scared by getting the hang of copywriting. Indeed, you are frequently your own most noticeably terrible faultfinder. As an entrepreneur, you have the information necessary to communicate best what it is you are endeavoring to sell and why it is significant for individuals to get it. Regardless of whether you offer an item, an administration, or both, nobody realizes your business superior to anything you do.

So how would you get familiar with the critical ability to a copywriter? Partake in copywriting training, for example, online courses, workshops, and instructional exercises. You are exploiting copywriting projects is an incredible method to focus on the most proficient way to compose internet duplicate, however how to utilize site copywriting to improve your business.

Copywriting projects can take you through the copywriting procedure, well ordered, helping you to create your message and best offer it with the online world. From separating your news and business from the challenge, to page builder software and copywriting study exercises, this is an incredible method to learn, ace and apply the specialty of productive and fruitful benefit delivering copywriting.

When you start getting the hang of copywriting and apply it to your online business, you will likewise observe precisely how significant it genuinely is. From composing a valid welcome message on your landing page to alluring your guests to select in and keeping them returning for additional, your Internet copywriting aptitudes will rapidly demonstrate to be an essential piece of your online business.

While picking up copywriting can be a test for some entrepreneurs, it is turning into an inexorably vital ability to get. It is critical to communicate effectively and productively, and the individuals who do it best are the individuals who succeed. When you have aced the ability of Internet copywriting, you will be a superior entrepreneur for it and your business will be progressively effective as a result of it. Try not to be scared. Internet copywriting can be simple if you set aside the effort to gain proficiency with the little-known techniques and recollect this one straightforward standard... You know your business, so compose what you know!

Why Freelance Copywriting is a Good Idea

Your business has been taking off and progressing admirably, and now you are thinking about contracting a full-time staff author. This unquestionably appears the following intelligent advance, however, there are a ton of included costs that accompany another perpetual representative added to your staff, (for example, office space, compensation, protection, preparing time and so on) that can without much of a stretch be kept away from.

How? By procuring a professional freelance copywriter. What's more, to set aside time and cash, however, to infuse some new point of view and new thoughts into your business also!

Freelance Efficiency

Outsourcing is proficient; it's as straightforward as that. It sets aside your time and cash and expands profitability. Re-appropriating your copywriting work to a freelance copywriter means getting a trained, experienced professional to deal with all your composition needs at much lower costs. In addition to the fact that they are devoted to just copywriting for you, yet they additionally do it on an as-required premise, sparing you paying for a worker's 'squander' time.

Further, freelancers are accessible at well beyond the regular 9-5 plan, enabling work to be done on a quick premise and sparing your time. They are additionally trained to deliver the most significant outcomes in minimum time, costing you even less in time than in cash, which can be crucial for those extremely incomprehensible due dates that yield up sometimes.

The Pro Freelancers

Professional freelancers will know precisely what to state, who to express it to, and how to say it. Your first message will be taken, cleaned up, idealized, and enunciated for the ideal outcomes. Regardless of whether it's your site content, a pamphlet or direct mail advertisement, an advertorial or just your business message, a professional freelance copywriter will enable you to build your benefits, online, and achievement. A right freelancer knows that an ideal duplicate, each time is the best way to accomplish a common win-win circumstance for the two gatherings.

Freelance copywriting won't just expand your profitability, bring down your expenses, and give you professionally composed duplicate, yet additionally, infuse new points of view into your business. Freelancer copywriters can take a shot at some hugely fluctuated and different activities that give them a full scope of experience and information to draw on when working for you. That additionally helps breathe new life into your business or the particular task, restoring your creative energies simultaneously.

Immaculate Copy, Every Time

The scientific approach of coordinating your item to the customer's purchasing procedure doesn't work in the generally 33% of all customers who are not guided by levelheaded choices. Goodness, gracious - what to do now?

Top Of The Pyramid: The 3 C's Approach

There is a superior method to prepare your business groups to sell your items. I've just chanced upon a bunch of item chiefs amid my vocation who have had the option to accomplish this dimension of a coordinated effort with their business groups. However, the achievement that they have had the opportunity to achieve has dependably filled in as an objective for me to shoot for.

At the highest point of the item selling method, the pyramid is the item troughs who demonstrate the business groups how they can collaborate with Customers to Create new items. The reasoning here is that a potential customer needs something other than your subject to take care of their problems. If you can instruct your business groups that your potential customers mostly don't have the foggiest idea what they don't have the foggiest idea and that they have to assist the customers with understanding the comprehensive view of an answer and how your item can fit into a general arrangement, at that point you'll have the option to make much more deals.

What All Of This Means For You

Item administrators are the CEO of your item. In your organization, you are the one individual who is most intensely put resources into the achievement of your item. All together for the thing to be fruitful, your business groups will need to realize how to offer it.

Very frequently item troughs do the base measure of work to get the business groups set up to sell their item: they diagram the item's advantages. What we have to do is to make the additional strides that will make our business groups much increasingly fruitful. This implies beginning by setting aside the effort to examine and comprehend our potential customer's purchasing propensities and examples. When we know these, at that point we can help our business groups coordinate them.

At last, we can work with deals to enable them to begin to team up more intimately with the customer. When they can do this, at that point, they'll have the option to open the ways to both more deals and more significant sales.

The most effective method to Manage Your Customers' Experience

The most effective method to deal with your customers' experience:

- Be open. There will be times when individuals need to talk with you as an issue of some direness. They may need to modify an arrangement, need to examine an adjustment in their necessities, feel constrained to share subtleties of something they're sad about.

When you're open individuals, come to see you as somebody who's anything but difficult to converse with, who's quick to do your best for them, who needs them to be content with your business and keep on utilizing your merchandise and ventures. When they feel upheld, they're sure about prescribing you to other people. Being neighborly and congenial stops issues exploding out of extent and turning into a major ordeal.

- Monitor online life. Numerous individuals utilize online presence, Twitter, Facebook, and so on to adulate as well as whine about the treatment they've gotten from organizations. I've perused someplace that an upbeat customer will educate three individuals concerning you while a sad one will tell eleven. Those figures become amplified when internet based life is ultimately used. Screen how you're being discussed, at that point you can respond rapidly to fix an issue, so transforming possibly terrible press into a decent PR result.

- Pretend to be your very own customer and find what it resembles to visit your business. The supervisory crew for my boisterous manufacturers said that they're office based and visit the site once every month! They depended on others to be their eyes and ears!

However, we need to be progressively proactive, a more significant number of hands-on than that, isn't that right? In light of that take a stab at calling your business with a and pitch it to customers, again and again. Some of the time it works, more often than not, it doesn't.

Moving To The Scientific Approach To Selling Your Product

Not all item supervisors are stuck at this essential dimension of supporting the business groups. A few of us have seen the mistakes of our ways and have figured out how to creep our way up to the following dimension: scientific selling support.

This is the place we've done some exploration (with or without the business group) to discover precisely how the customer approaches settling on purchasing choices - what is their purchasing procedure.

This approach, for the most part, gets a lot a more significant number of offers that the old method for directly pitching the item's incentive to whatever number customers as could reasonably be expected. There is one problem: not all customers are balanced.

At long last, the ideal duplicate referenced above; professionally done freelance copywriting will be without blunder and eloquent. No grammatical mistakes, spelling blunders or linguistic missteps; the freelance copywriter will give you elegantly composed and thoroughly edited duplicate without fail, sparing you on both time expenses and shame. It's a success win circumstance for you and them - what are you sitting tight for?

How to "read your customers' minds," and get them looking for reasons to buy from you

When you need a sound bite for what we're doing, at that point it would be the "pitch and implore" procedure. This is the place we instruct the business groups about the estimation of our item and afterward have them go out

raise inquiries or solicitation more data that will assist them with writing the following draft.

that smart thoughts can emerge out of anyplace, so they wouldn't fret sharing the credit.

Sometime in the distant past, the copywriter may have presented their work to the client through fax or even mail. These days they will, for the most part, send the first draft as a Word report connected to an email.

For some, freelance copywriters, meeting the client is a rare event, and in actuality, it is ending up increasingly more typical for freelance copywriters to work with clients that they have never met or even addressed by telephone. While this can make the freelance copywriter feel somewhat segregated, it brings the advantage of enabling them to work with clients who are found anyplace on the planet. It can likewise be made communication between client and copywriter snappier and progressively proficient.

If proper, the freelance copywriter may send remarks alongside their composition, either in the content itself or in a going with email. This causes the client to comprehend the setting of the choices that the freelance copywriter has made, just as enabling the copywriter to

Many copywriting undertakings can be finished by a copywriter working alone. Others require a dimension of association and collaborating to deliver the best duplicate. Adverts, for instance, once in a while relying upon copywriting alone for their effect: the best advertisements are made by a copywriter working in an organization with an inventive fashioner or craftsmanship chief, perhaps upheld by a client account director who speaks to the client's desires and needs. This kind of setup is no doubt in an office plan. The copywriter and craftsmanship executive work firmly together, perhaps brainstorming ideas and refining them in the organization before teaming up in the real generation of the advertisement.

When the genuine innovative substance is being made, the copywriter assumes liability for the words, while the craftsmanship chief thinks about what pictures or designs will best pass on the message. In any case, the two jobs can and should cover: great copywriters will frequently propose plans or photos to go with their words, while experienced craftsmanship chiefs may thoroughly recommend a 'picture in addition to motto' thought. In this circumstance, it's down to the master in every region to affirm that the idea is sound and refine it beyond what many would consider possible. Talented creatives realize or convincing idea jumps out at them, they can write it down and guarantee it gets utilized.

It's a sheltered supposition that most freelance copywriters are presently utilizing Microsoft Word or a comparable word-preparing program for their composition. The sheer usability in having the option to compose, rework, and rebuild your work makes this an easy decision for most by far of freelance copywriters. In any case, many do want to utilize pen and paper for specific assignments, extraordinarily very innovative or short-duplicate work, for example, composing organization slogans or publicizing mottos. PCs offer a broad scope of diversions for the freelance copywriter, for example, browsing their email or refreshing an online profile, and it tends to merit making tracks in the opposite direction from these to concentrate on the center assignment of exploratory writing.

Most freelance copywriters will experience a few emphases of their composition before sending anything to their client, ordinarily evacuating a lot of composing that isn't required before they present their first draft. It could be contended that the essential skill of the copywriter isn't making content, however removing the composition that isn't required.

they talk about their administrations or items? Who comes first, the organization or the client?

People are generally narcissistic; it's in our temperament to take care of 'number one.' For business purposes this should be flipped completely around: you have to consider your identity pitching to, as opposed to slamming into about how incredible you are. Clients don't give a tinker's toot about your business; they just consideration about how might this benefit them. How are they going to profit from your item or administrations? Will their lives be improved, and by what amount? Will they get an incentive for cash?

This idea ought to be predominant in the entirety of your visual marketing: site, limited time writing, publicizing, shop front, stock, organizing: pitch, introduction and social online, deals patter with your clients - in certainty any visual outlet of your organization. The client dependably starts things out, as it is they you are elevating to, and it is they who will come at last purchase.

Another factor to consider is time. Try not to go frantic endeavoring to clarify everything, mainly if it's genuinely dull stuff about your organization. The 21st century is a

Go to trade shows for your product specialty. This is a suitable method to perceive what purchasers are searching for and what flow and future products they are excited for. Go to seminars or workshops that your opposition might hold. Sit and tune in to the speaker as they talk about their business. Focus on the orderlies as they pose inquiries and tune in to the speaker's reaction. Make sure you accept high notes as you may gain proficiency with another methodology or strategy concerning your product specialty. Go to networking meetings held by nearby and national organizations. You can shape joint venture partnerships with your opposition and influence their present purchaser's rundown for your products.

The most effective method to Use Your Customers to Promote Your Business

Clients are critical to your business, where might it be without them? This may sound self-evident. However, there are a few businesses that trundle along failing to acknowledge this essential component.

When examining a business advancement, consider to whom they are conversing with. Who is the fundamental goal in their marketing message? Who is set at the highest point of their promoting? Who are they depicting when doesn't occur time and again, you'll see that you keep up excellent relations with your customers and can keep them cheerful.

Treat others as you might want to be dealt with is a recognizable saying that has a specific vibration when you're managing a customer or customer. Accepting these tips can empower you to deal with the positive, successful customer experience and keep everybody glad.

Step by step instructions to Anticipate Your Customer's Buying Needs and Generate More Product Sales

For what reason do fortune 500 organizations make it to that dimension of glory? Is it since they have a decent product? Is it as a result of their superb client administration? Or on the other hand, perhaps they have an eminent business framework? While these might be the correct answer, your client devotion will originate from foreseeing their needs and giving the arrangements fundamental. You can ask any online entrepreneur, and they'll let you know, living up to your client's desires are little peanuts contrasted with foreseeing their needs and reacting rapidly to them. You should most likely read the request, an inquiry, a grumbling or utilize a mystery customer to visit your premises to perceive how clean, valid, benevolent the administration is. That way, you stay mindful of what a typical customer experience resembles.

- Communicate what's happening in your business. Familiarize your customers and customers with any progressions to staff, trading hours, terms, and conditions. Give away accommodating tips and exhortation. Possibly give occasional offers and customer prizes to keep your customers boosted. Give preparing days or workshops to encourage your customers with better aptitudes. Lead the pack, thus deal with your customers' experience.

- If things aren't going very right or are notwithstanding turning out badly for a customer, assume liability, let it be known straight away and after that, you can begin to talk about compelling approaches to fix things. The vast majority are sensible when they are managed deferentially.

They are transparent about mistakes or exclusions as quickly as time permits take into consideration them to be managed in an ideal manner for all concerned. Since it organization. They request related products, start to make those products and give it to them. If they are making recommendations on the best way to improve your products, do what you have to improve. If they are leaving you mean remarks about how awful your product sucks, fix the issue right away!

3. Keep bird of prey eyes on your opposition.

It's an unquestionable requirement that you watch out for your opposition. For what reason do you think pro game groups watch the film on their opposition? They do this to think about their plays to perceive what they progress nicely and to exploit their defects. You should do likewise with your opponent! See what sort of products they are giving, ending, raising costs on, putting at a bargain, and so on. This is a suitable method to see "what's hot" and what their clients are looking for. A smart thought is joining your rival's newsletter, and mailing list as this is a decent method to remain instructed and modern!

4. Go to trade shows, seminars, organizations, or shows.

brains of your clients so you can make sense of what they need and give the correct apparatuses and products to satisfy their needs. When you don't do it, your opposition will. That implies lost income for you, ouch!

Here are four basic approaches to think about your client's needs:

1. Investigate the details of your immediate sale.

Give close consideration to the buys your clients are right now making through your site. You'll need to see who is purchasing what and how a lot of cash clients are spending on each request. You may likewise need to follow which website pages they are investing the most energy in and to what extent they're remaining on your webpage.

2. Monitor client's inquiries, recommendations, and remarks.

I couldn't care less if clients are speaking with your business by telephone, email, or web accommodation structure; monitor their interchanges with your

The 'unintentional' street to turning into a master copywriter could without much of a stretch emerge from a progression of commissions from an office (or another customer) which incidentally constructs a decent portfolio in a specific sector or copywriting, (for example, regular postal mail).

Associations that utilization copywriting administrations regularly need to choose whether to utilize a pro or non-authority, even though this relies upon their line of business (in addition to other things). There's a deep division between business-to-business and purchaser/FMCG copywriters. The methodology that is required is altogether different, albeit some would state that definitive finishes are the equivalent, in particular, to influence people to make specific courses of the move.

Organizations in the innovation and other prosectors will properly search out writers with significant experience. As with such a large number of businesses, having insider learning of the market, the language and what motivates people to connect with you - this shows in duplicate. Talking a similar style as your intended interest group is a fundamental pre-imperative of promoting achievement.

For organizations of pretty much every sort, the Internet gives an enormous selection of copywriters, each with their very own aptitudes, experience, and charge levels. For copywriters themselves, the open doors have never been more prominent - nor has the dimension of rivalry.

Free market activity is changing the structure of the copywriting market. The interest in online substance is tremendous, and this has made a multitude of 'entrepreneur' copywriters with constrained understanding or ability. Luckily, exceptionally talented copywriting will dependably be required overall business sectors. As ever, the future will develop with market powers.

The most effective method to Get Copywriting Jobs - What Style Attracts Your Readers

In case you're searching for counsel on what specific composition styles to use for your copywriting jobs, at that point you need entirely to peruse this whole part.